enVisionmath 2.0

Volume 1B Topics 5–8

Authors

Randall I. Charles
Professor Emeritus
Department of Mathematics
San Jose State University
San Jose, California

Jennifer Bay-Williams
Professor of Mathematics Education
College of Education and Human
Development
University of Louisville
Louisville, Kentucky

Robert Q. Berry, III
Associate Professor of
Mathematics Education
Department of Curriculum,
Instruction and Special Education
University of Virginia
Charlottesville, Virginia

Janet H. Caldwell
Professor of Mathematics
Rowan University
Glassboro, New Jersey

Zachary Champagne
Assistant in Research
Florida Center for Research in Science,
Technology, Engineering, and
Mathematics (FCR-STEM)
Jacksonville, Florida

Juanita Copley
Professor Emerita, College of Education
University of Houston
Houston, Texas

Warren Crown
Professor Emeritus of Mathematics
Education
Graduate School of Education
Rutgers University
New Brunswick, New Jersey

Francis (Skip) Fennell
L. Stanley Bowlsbey Professor
of Education and Graduate and
Professional Studies
McDaniel College
Westminster, Maryland

Karen Karp
Professor of Mathematics Education
Department of Early Childhood and
Elementary Education
University of Louisville
Louisville, Kentucky

Stuart J. Murphy
Visual Learning Specialist
Boston, Massachusetts

Jane F. Schielack
Professor of Mathematics
Associate Dean for Assessment and
Pre K–12 Education, College of Science
Texas A&M University
College Station, Texas

Jennifer M. Suh
Associate Professor for
Mathematics Education
George Mason University
Fairfax, Virginia

Jonathan A. Wray
Mathematics Instructional Facilitator
Howard County Public Schools
Ellicott City, Maryland

SAVVAS
LEARNING COMPANY

Mathematicians

Roger Howe
Professor of Mathematics
Yale University
New Haven, Connecticut

Gary Lippman
Professor of Mathematics and
Computer Science
California State University, East Bay
Hayward, California

ELL Consultants

Janice R. Corona
Independent Education Consultant
Dallas, Texas

Jim Cummins
Professor
The University of Toronto
Toronto, Canada

Debbie Crisco
Math Coach
Beebe Public Schools
Beebe, Arkansas

Kathleen A. Cuff
Teacher
Kings Park Central School District
Kings Park, New York

Erika Doyle
Math and Science Coordinator
Richland School District
Richland, Washington

Reviewers

Susan Jarvis
Math and Science Curriculum Coordinator
Ocean Springs Schools
Ocean Springs, Mississippi

SAVVAS
LEARNING COMPANY

ISBN-13: 978-0-328-93059-3
ISBN-10:   0-328-93059-8
6 2022

Solve Learn Glossary

Tools Assessment Help Games

TOPIC 5 — Classify and Count Data

Essential Question: How can classifying data help answer questions?

Some cows are brown and some are black.

Cows can be different colors.

Math and Science Project: Sorting Animals

Directions Read the character speech bubbles to students. **Find Out!** Have students find out about animals that can be organized by color.
Say: *Talk to friends and relatives about animals. Talk about how an animal can be one color, but another of the same animal can be a different color.*
Journal: Make a Poster Have students make a poster. Have them choose one animal they learned about, and then draw a group of 6–10 animals. Ask them to color the animals using two different colors, and then write the numbers to tell how many of each color.

Topic 5   two hundred forty-five **245**

Name _____

Review What You Know

1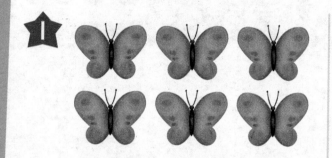

2

3

4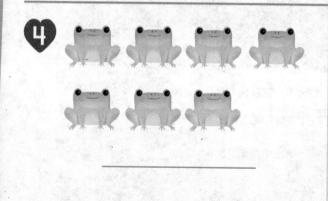

_____

_ _ _ _ _ _ _ _ _ _ _ _

5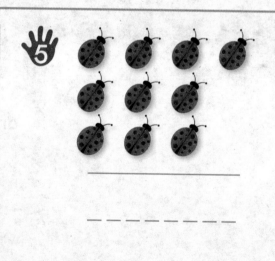

_ _ _ _ _ _ _ _ _ _ _ _

6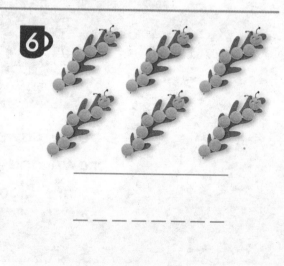

_ _ _ _ _ _ _ _ _ _ _ _

Directions Have students: **1** draw a circle around the group with 10 bugs; **2** draw a circle around the group that has a number of birds that is less than 5; **3** draw a circle around the group that has a number of birds that is greater than 5; **4**–**6** count the frogs or bugs in each group, and then write the number to tell how many.

My Word Cards

A-Z
Glossary

category	**classify**	**chart**
tally mark		

My Word Cards

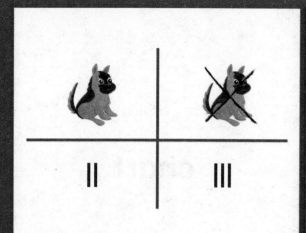

Point to the chart.
Say: *A **chart** is where information is organized.*

Point to the cats.
Say: *To **classify** objects is to sort them into categories. These are all cats.*

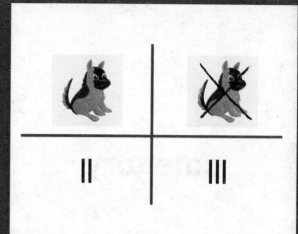

Point to the dog category.
Say: *A **category** groups things by similar attributes.*

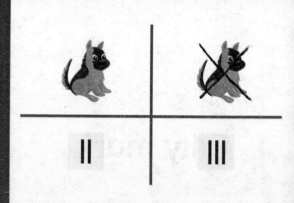

Point to the tally marks.
Say: *A **tally mark** is a mark that helps record data. I mark represents I object.*

4 legs

NOT 4 legs

Pet Fair

Directions Say: *Carlos's kindergarten class is having a pet fair. The pets need to be put into two tents. One tent is for pets with 4 legs. The other tent is for pets that do NOT have 4 legs. Draw pictures of 5 pets. Where should you put them? How do you know you put them in the right tent?*

I can ...
classify objects into categories and tell why they are in each category.

I can also reason about math.

Hair

NO Hair

Classify.

☆ Guided Practice

1

Directions 1 Have students draw a circle around the animals that have feathers, and then mark an X on the animals that do NOT have feathers.

Topic 5 | Lesson 1

Directions ② **Math and Science** Say: *What can most animals with wings do?* Have students draw a circle around the animals that have wings, and then mark an X on the animals that do NOT have wings. Have students: ③ draw a circle around the rabbits that are white, and then mark an X on the rabbits that are NOT white; ④ draw a circle around the cows that are brown, and then mark an X on the cows that are NOT brown; ⑤ draw a circle around the dogs that have spots, and then mark an X on the dogs that do NOT have spots.

Independent Practice

Directions Have students: ❻ draw a circle around the birds that are green, and then mark an X on the birds that are NOT green; ❼ draw a circle around the animals that have tails, and then mark an X on the animals that do NOT have tails. ❽ **Higher Order Thinking** Say: *The animals have been classified into two categories. How were the animals classified?* Have students draw a picture of an animal that belongs in each category.

Topic 5 | Lesson 1

Name _____

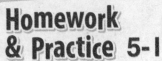
Homework & Practice 5-1
Classify Objects into Categories

Another Look!

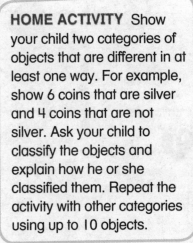

HOME ACTIVITY Show your child two categories of objects that are different in at least one way. For example, show 6 coins that are silver and 4 coins that are not silver. Ask your child to classify the objects and explain how he or she classified them. Repeat the activity with other categories using up to 10 objects.

Directions Say: *You can classify objects into categories and tell how you classified them. Draw a circle around the animals that are adults, and then mark an X on the animals that are NOT adults.* ⭐ Have students draw a circle around the animals that have beaks, and then mark an X on the animals that do NOT have beaks.

2

3

4

Directions Have students: **2** draw a circle around the animals that are spotted, and then mark an X on the animals that are NOT spotted; **3** draw a circle around the fish that are yellow, and then mark an X on the fish that are NOT yellow. **4** **Higher Order Thinking** Say: *The mice are classified into two categories. One group has cheese and the other group does NOT have cheese. What is another way you could classify the mice?* Have students draw pictures to show how they could classify the mice in another way.

Topic 5 | **Lesson 1**

Name _____

Solve

_____

- - - - - - - -

_____

On the ground

_____

- - - - - - - -

_____

NOT on the ground

Directions Say: *Carlos goes outside and sees some creatures. How many creatures does he see on the ground? How many does he see that are NOT on the ground? Tell how you know you counted all of the creatures.*

I can ... count how many objects are in different categories.

I can also be precise in my work.

Count.

☆ Guided Practice

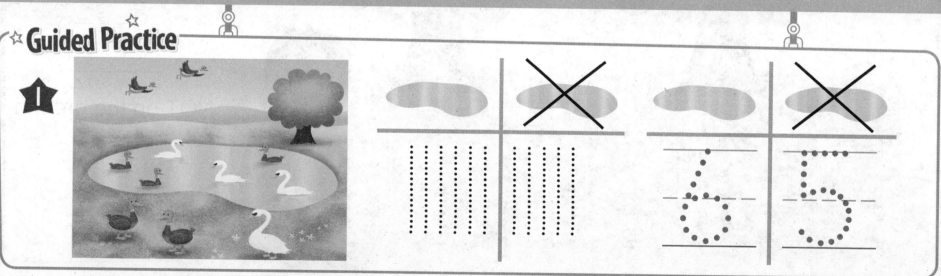

Directions ⭐ Have students draw lines in the chart as they count the animals that are in the pond and the animals that are NOT in the pond, and then write the numbers to tell how many in another chart.

Topic 5 | Lesson 2

Name _____

2

3

Directions **2 Vocabulary** Have students draw lines in the chart as they count the animals that have 8 legs and the animals that do NOT have 8 legs, and then write the numbers to tell how many are in each **category** in another chart. **3** Have students draw lines in the chart as they count the birds that are in the trees and the birds that are NOT in the trees, and then write the numbers to tell how many are in each category in another chart.

Independent Practice

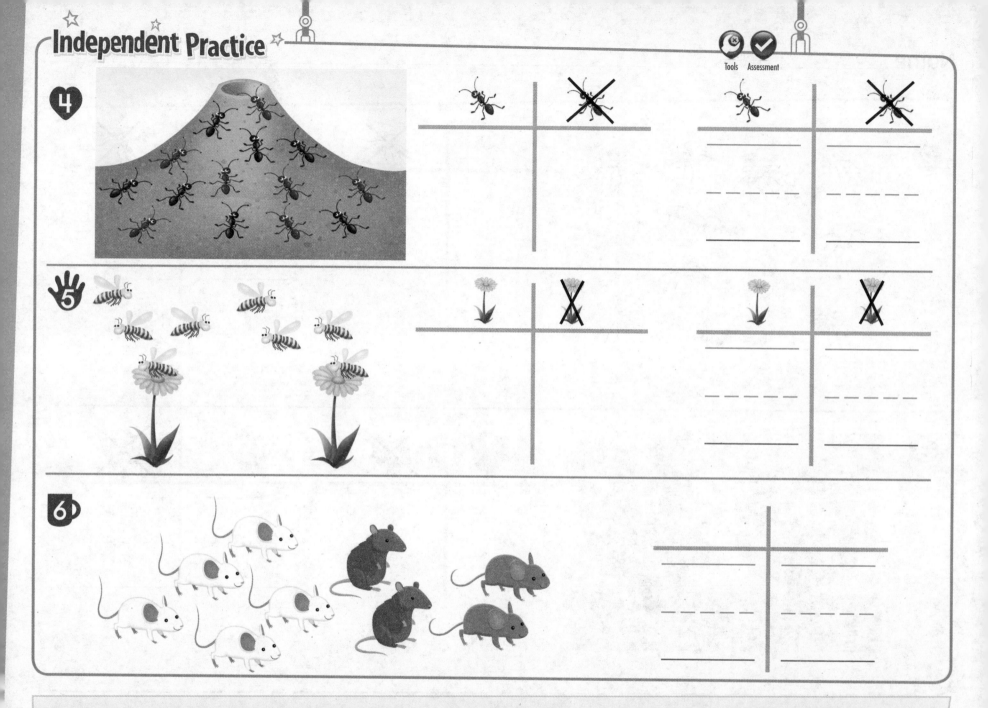

Directions   Have students: ❹ draw lines in the chart as they count the ants that are red and the ants that are NOT red, and then write the numbers to tell how many in another chart; ❺ draw lines in the chart as they count the bees that are on flowers and the bees that are NOT on flowers, and then write the numbers to tell how many in another chart. ❻ **Higher Order Thinking** Say: *These mice are sorted into two categories. How are they sorted?* Have students draw a picture in the chart to show the categories, and then write the numbers to tell how many mice are in each category.

     Topic 5 | Lesson 2

Name _____

Another Look!

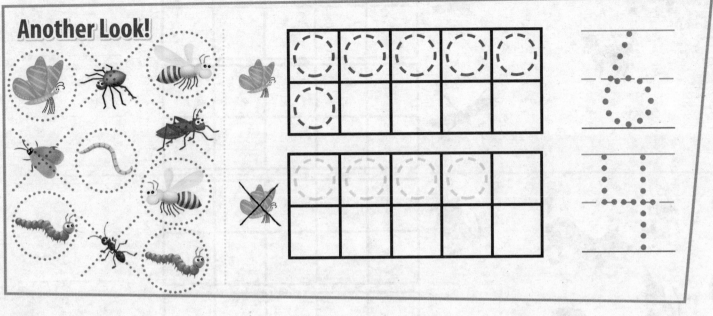

HOME ACTIVITY Show your child a group of 12 or fewer objects that are different in at least one way. For example, show 4 blue buttons, 3 brown buttons, and 5 white buttons. Arrange the objects in a random order. Ask your child to draw lines to count the buttons that are white and the buttons that are NOT white. Then have your child write numbers for his or her lines. Repeat the activity with other categories of up to 12 objects.

Directions Say: *You can use counters and a ten-frame to sort objects and count how many objects are in each category. Draw a circle around each animal that has stripes. Draw that many red counters in the top ten-frame, and then write the number to tell how many. Mark an X on each animal that does NOT have stripes. Draw that many yellow counters in the bottom ten-frame, and then write the number to tell how many.* ⭐ Have students draw a circle around each animal that has 4 legs, draw that many red counters in the top ten-frame, and then write the number to tell how many. Have students mark an X on each animal that does NOT have 4 legs, draw that many yellow counters in the bottom ten-frame, and then write the number to tell how many.

Directions Have students draw a circle around animals in one category, draw that many red counters in the top ten-frame, and then write the number to tell how many. Then have them mark an X on animals in the other category, draw that many yellow counters in the bottom ten-frame, and then write the number to tell how many. ❷ Categories: animals that have wings, animals that do NOT have wings ❸ Categories: dogs that are puppies, dogs that are NOT puppies. ❹ **Higher Order Thinking** Say: *Gretchen is going to put 1 more striped fish in the aquarium. Draw red counters in the top ten-frame to show how many striped fish will be in the aquarium. Write the number to tell how many.* Have students mark an X on the fish that are NOT striped, draw yellow counters in the bottom ten-frame, and then write the number to tell how many.

Name _____

Directions Say: *Carlos's kindergarten class has a new playground area. Sort the new playground into toys that have wheels and toys that do NOT have wheels. Draw a circle around the category that is greater than the other category. Tell how you know.*

I can ...
use counting to compare how many objects are in categories.

I can also be precise in my work.

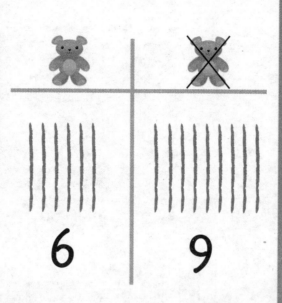

6 9

1 2 3 4 5 6 7 8 9 10

☆ Guided Practice

1

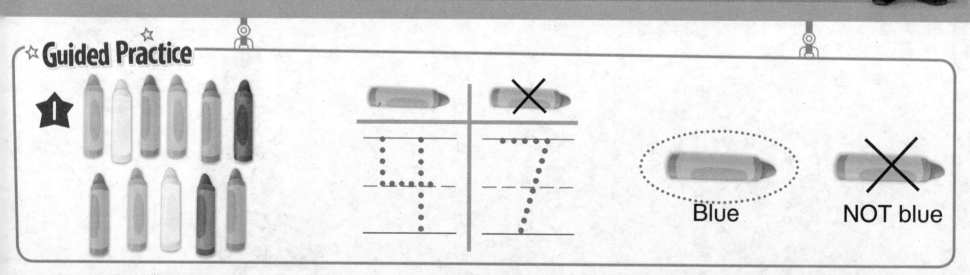

Blue   NOT blue

Directions ⭐ Have students sort the crayons into crayons that are blue and crayons that are NOT blue, count them, and then write numbers in the chart to tell how many. Have students draw a circle around the category that is less in number than the other category and tell how they know.

262 two hundred sixty-two

Topic 5 | Lesson 3

2

3

Directions Have students: **2** sort the blocks into blocks that have letters and blocks that do NOT have letters, count them, and then write numbers in the chart to tell how many. Then have students draw a circle around the category that is greater in number than the other category and tell how they know; **3** sort the books into books that are open and books that are NOT open, count them, and then write numbers in the chart to tell how many. Then have students draw a circle around the category that is less in number than the other category and tell how they know.

Independent Practice

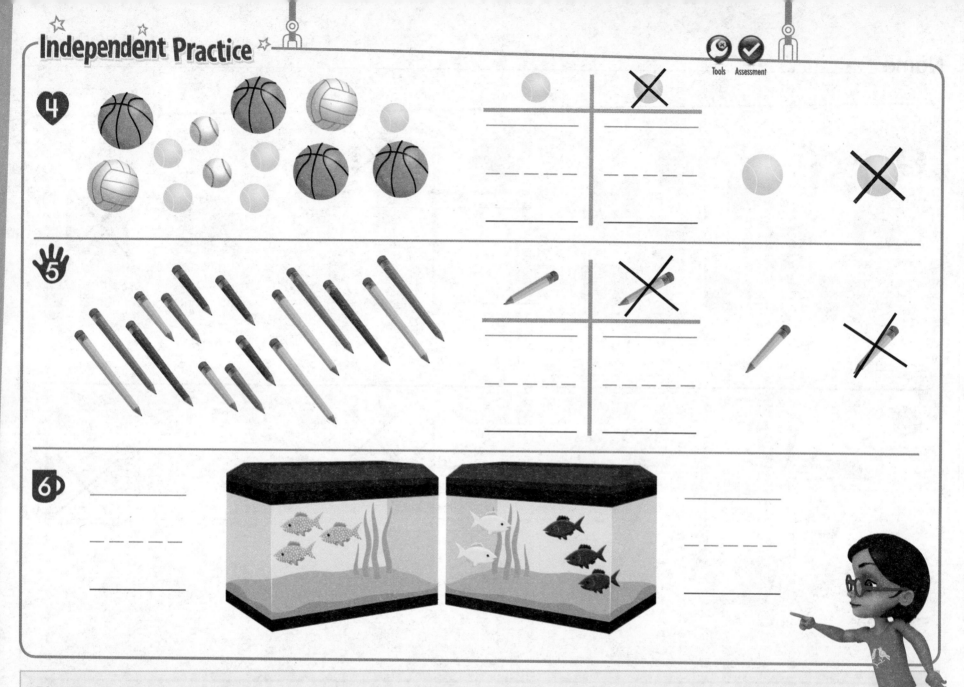

4

5

6

Directions Have students: **4** sort the balls into balls that are yellow and balls that are NOT yellow, count them, and then write numbers in the chart to tell how many. Then have students draw a circle around the category that is greater in number than the other category and tell how they know; **5** sort the pencils into pencils that are short and pencils that are NOT short, count them, and then write numbers in the chart to tell how many. Then have students draw a circle around the category that is greater in number than the other category and tell how they know. **6 Higher Order Thinking** Say: *The fish are sorted into fish that have spots and fish that do NOT have spots.* Have students draw fish so the categories have an equal number of fish, and then write the number of fish in each category. Ask: *How do you know the categories have an equal number of fish?*

Topic 5 | Lesson 3

Name _____

Another Look!

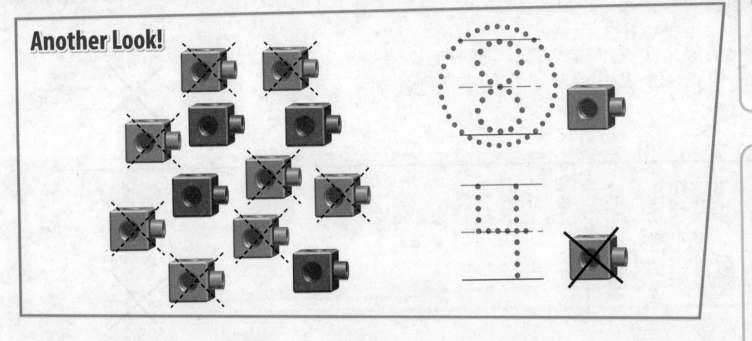

HOME ACTIVITY Show your child a group of 12 or fewer objects that are different in at least one way. For example, show 5 spoons and 6 forks. Arrange them in a random order. Ask your child to count the objects that are forks and the objects that are NOT forks, tell which category has a greater number of objects, and then explain how he or she knows. Repeat with another group of objects and have your child tell you which category has a number of objects that is less than the other category.

⭐ 1

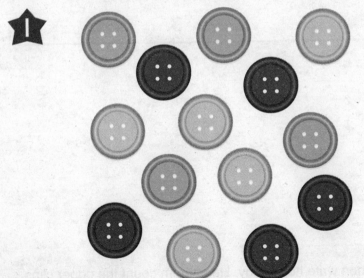

_____

- - - - - -

_____

_____

_____

- - - - - -

_____

Directions Say: *Mark an X on the blue cubes, count the blue cubes, and then write how many. Count the cubes that are NOT blue, and then write how many. Draw a circle around the number that is greater than the other number. Tell how you know.* ⭐ Have students mark an X on each purple button, count them, and then write how many. Have students count the buttons that are NOT purple, write how many, and then draw a circle around the number that is less than the other number. Have them tell how they know.

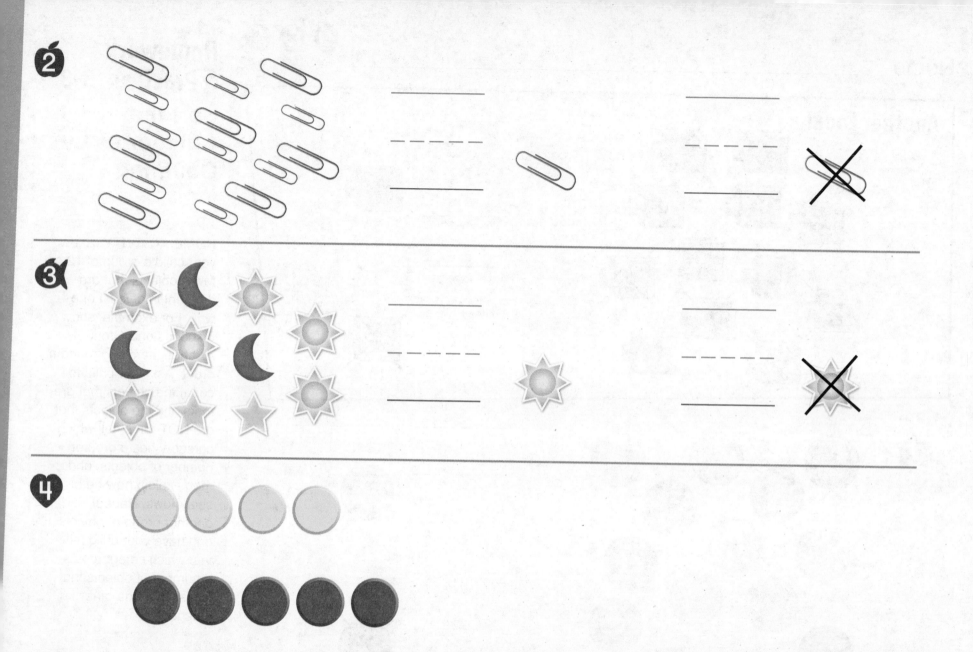

Directions ② Have students mark an X on each large paper clip, count them, and then write how many. Have them count the paper clips that are NOT large, and then write how many. Then have students draw a circle around the number that is greater, and then tell how they know. ③ **Number Sense** Have students mark an X on each sticker that is a sun, count them, and then write how many. Have students count the stickers that are NOT suns, and then write how many. Then have them draw a circle around the number that is greater, and then tell how they know. ④ **Higher Order Thinking** Say: *These counters are sorted into red counters and counters that are NOT red.* Have students draw yellow counters so that the number of yellow counters is greater in number than the counters that are NOT yellow, and then tell how they know.

Topic 5 | Lesson 3

Name _____

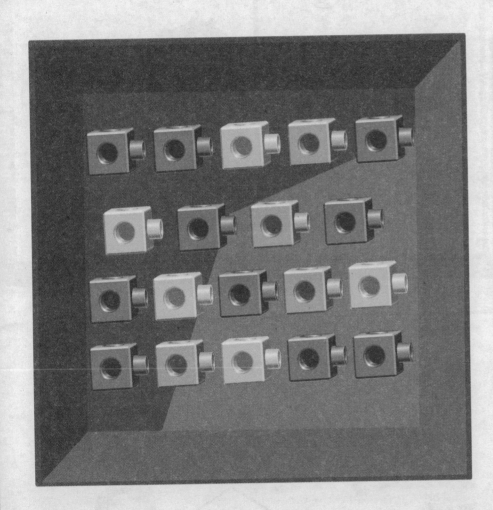

Think.

I can ...
tell whether the way objects
have been sorted, counted,
and compared makes sense.
I can explain how I know.

I can also compare
numbers.

Directions Say: *Carlos says that the number of blue cubes is equal to the number of cubes that are NOT blue. Does his answer make sense? Use numbers, pictures, or words to explain your answer.*

Which is correct?

Name <u>Tucker</u>

6   5

↑

Name <u>Olivia</u>

6   (5)

1 2 3 4 (5) 6 7 8 9 10
        ↑

Both answers are correct.

☆ Guided Practice

1   yes

no

5
6

Directions ❶ Say: *Gabbi says that the category of airplanes is greater in number than the category that is NOT airplanes. Does her answer make sense?* Have students draw a circle around *yes* or *no*, and then use the sorting and counting of each category to explain their reasoning.

Topic 5 | Lesson 4

Name _____

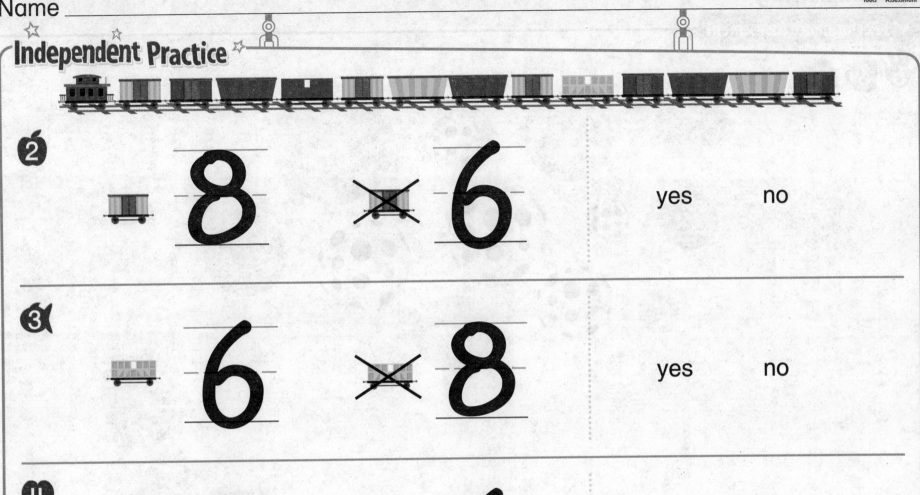

Independent Practice

2 8 ✗ 6   yes   no

3 6 ✗ 8   yes   no

4 8 ✗ 6   yes   no

Directions Have students listen to each problem, draw a circle around *yes* or *no*, and then use the sorting and counting of each category to explain their reasoning. **2** *Damon says that he counted 8 yellow train cars and 6 train cars that are NOT yellow. Does his answer make sense?* **3** *Malinda says that the category of yellow train cars is less than the category of train cars that are NOT yellow. Does her answer make sense?* **4** *Aaron says that the category of red train cars is greater than the category of train cars that are NOT red. Does his answer make sense?*

Topic 5 | Lesson 4   two hundred sixty-nine **269**

Directions Read the problem aloud. Then have students use multiple problem-solving methods to solve the problem. Say: *Alex says that if there was 1 fewer orange ball, then the category of orange balls would be equal in number to the category of balls that are NOT orange. Does his answer make sense?* ✋ **Reasoning** *Think about it. How many orange balls would there be if there was 1 fewer orange ball?* Use numbers, tools, or draw a picture to show how many orange balls there would be. ☕ **Be Precise** *Is the number of orange balls equal to the number of balls that are NOT orange?* 🌲 **Critique Reasoning** *Use the sorting and counting of each category to explain your reasoning.*

Topic 5 | Lesson 4

Name _____

Help   Tools   Games

Homework & Practice 5-4

Critique Reasoning

Another Look!

 6 **×7**   (yes)   no

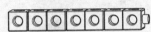

⭐ **5** × **8**   yes   no

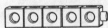

HOME ACTIVITY Show your child a group of up to 19 objects that are different in at least one way; for example, 9 plates and 8 cups. Arrange the objects in a random order and make a statement comparing the objects. For example, say: *The category of plates is greater than the category of cups.* Ask your child whether your statement makes sense and to explain how he or she knows. Repeat the activity with other groups of objects and statements that either make sense or do NOT make sense.

Directions Say: *Tanya used cubes to show how many crayons are yellow and how many crayons are NOT yellow. She says that the category of yellow crayons is less in number than the category of crayons that are NOT yellow. Does her answer make sense? Draw a circle around* yes *or* no. *Then use the sorting and counting of each category to explain their reasoning.* ⭐ Say: *Jared says that the category of green crayons is greater than the category that is NOT green. Does his answer make sense?* Then have students draw a circle around *yes* or *no*, and then use the sorting and counting of each category to explain their reasoning.

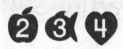

Directions Read the problem aloud. Then have students use multiple problem-solving methods to solve the problem. Say: *Carlos says that if there were 3 more brown dogs, then the category of brown dogs would be greater in number than the category of dogs that are NOT brown. He uses cubes to show the categories of dogs. Does his answer make sense?* ❷ **Model** *How can you show whether or not his answer makes sense? Use tools or draw a picture to show how many brown dogs there would be if 3 more brown dogs join the category.* ❸ **Be Precise** *Is the number of brown dogs now greater than the number of dogs that are NOT brown?* ❹ **Critique Reasoning** *Use the sorting and counting of each category to explain your reasoning.*

Name _____

Vocabulary Review

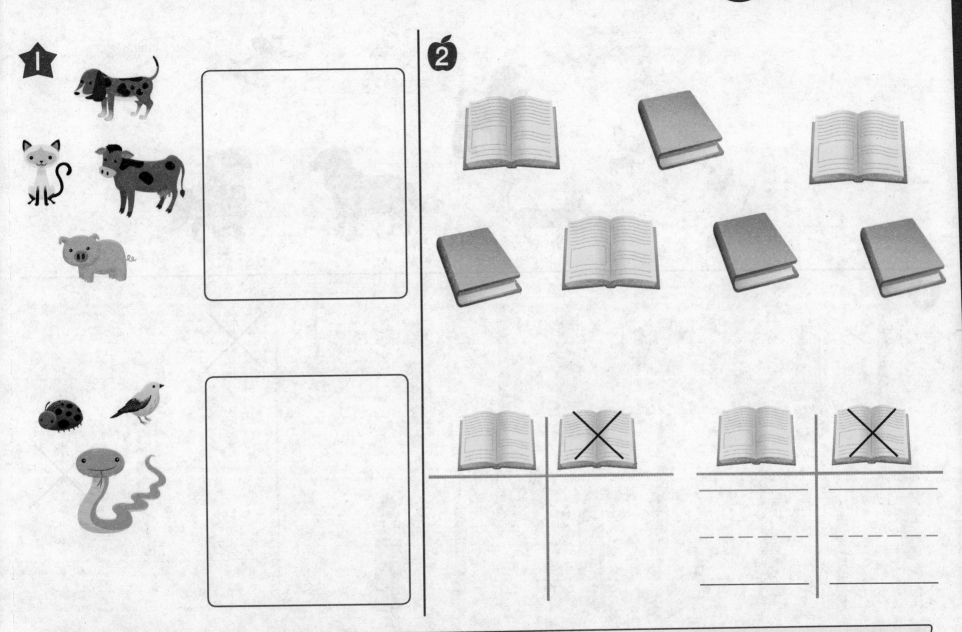

Directions **Understand Vocabulary** Have students: ⭐ draw an animal that fits each **category**, and then tell how the groups are organized; 🍎 sort books into books that are open and books that are NOT open. Have them draw **tally marks** in the chart as they count, and then write the number in another chart.

Topic 5 | Vocabulary Review
two hundred seventy-three **273**

3

4

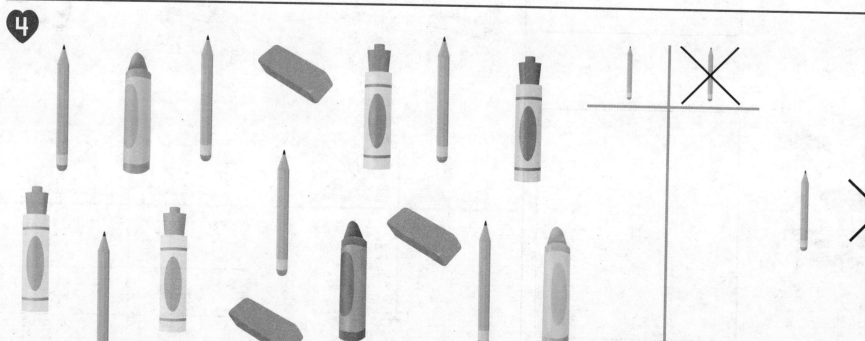

Set A

Set B

Directions Have students: ❶ draw a circle around the animals that walk on 2 legs, and then mark an X on the animals that do NOT walk on 2 legs; ❷ draw lines in the chart as they count the toys that are on the rug and the toys that are NOT on the rug. Then have them write the numbers to tell how many are in each group in another chart.

Set C

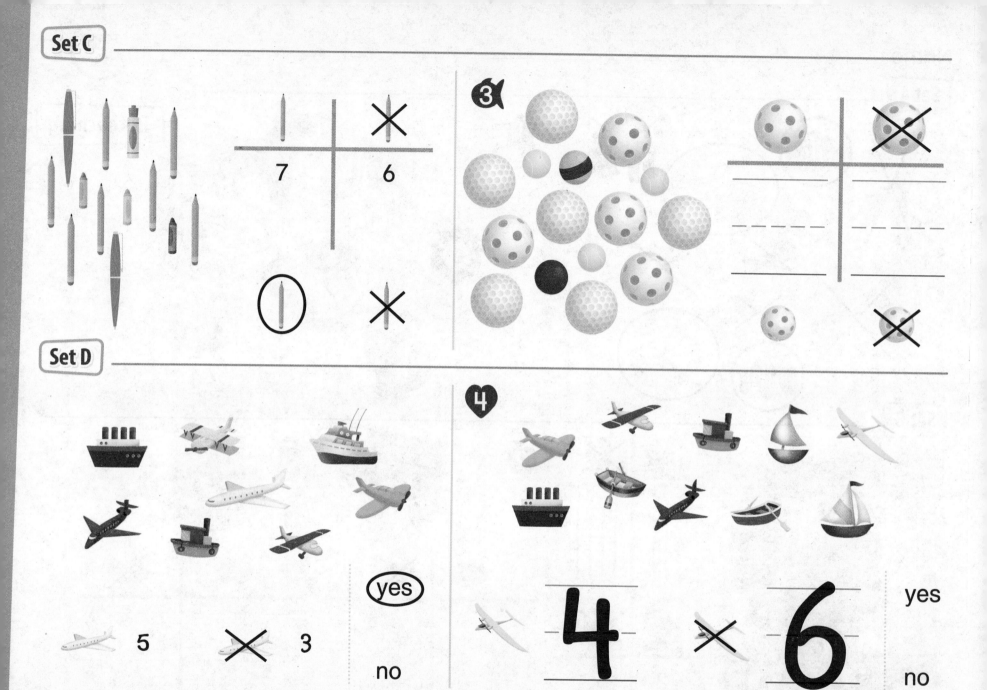

3

7	✗ 6
Ⓞ	✗

Set D

4

✈ 5   ✗ 3   yes / no

4 ✗ 6   yes / no

Name _____

1

Ⓐ Ⓒ Ⓑ Ⓓ

2

☐ ☐ ☐ ☐

3

Directions Have students mark the best answer. ★ Which chart shows how many fish are yellow and how many fish are NOT yellow?
❷ Say: *The animals have been classified into two categories. Mark all the animals that belong in the category of animals inside the circle.*
❸ Have students draw a circle around the animals that fly, and mark an X on the animals that do NOT fly.

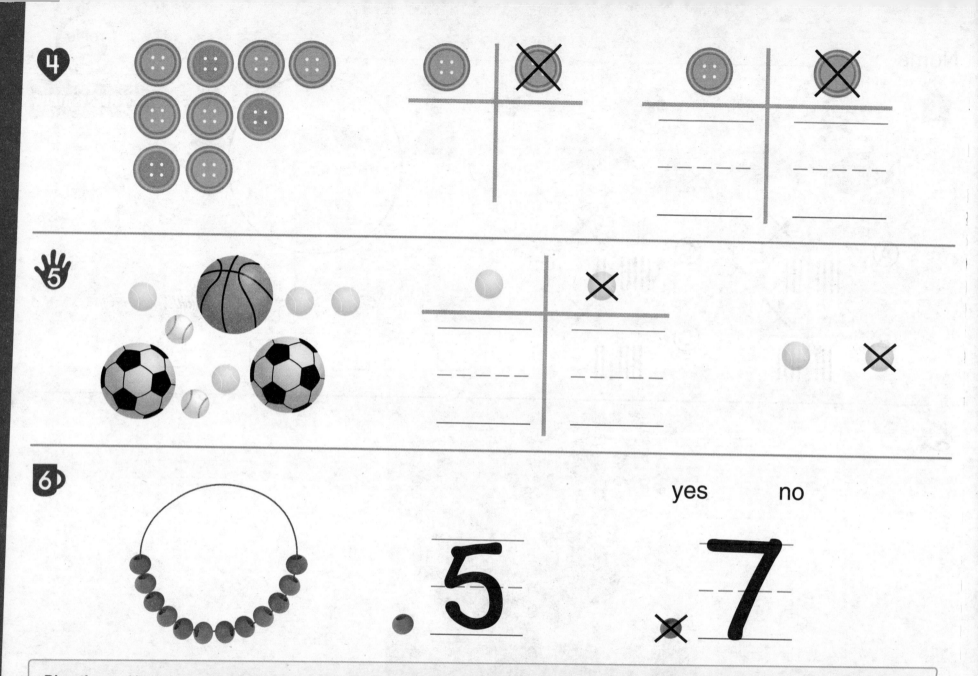

yes   no

$.5$

$\times 7$

Directions Have students: ♥ draw lines in the chart as they count the buttons that are green and the buttons that are NOT green, and then write the numbers to tell how many in another chart; ✋ sort the balls into balls that are tennis balls and balls that are NOT tennis balls, count them, and then write numbers in the chart to tell how many. Then have students draw a circle around the category that is less in number than the other category; ☕ listen to the problem, draw a circle around *yes* or *no*, and then use numbers, pictures, or words to explain how they know whether the answer makes sense. Say: *Dana says that the category of blue beads is greater in number than the category of beads that are NOT blue. Does her answer make sense?*

Topic 5 | Assessment

Name _____

★1

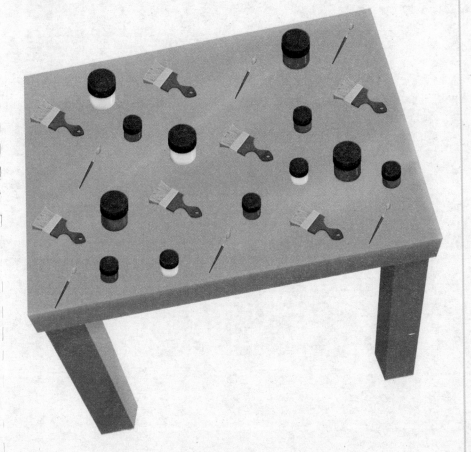

2

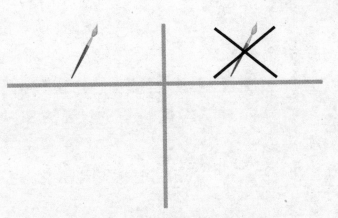

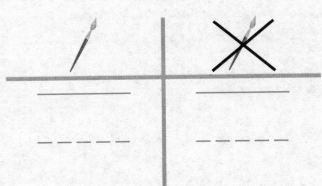

Directions **Works of Art** Say: *A kindergarten class uses paintbrushes and paint to draw pictures.* Have students: **★** draw a circle around the little paintbrushes, and then mark an X over the paintbrushes that are NOT little; **2** draw lines in the first chart as they count the paintbrushes that are little and the paintbrushes that are NOT little. Then have them write the number to tell how many are in each group in the second chart, and draw a circle around the number of the group that is less than the number of the other group.

yes   no

TOPIC 6 Understand Addition

Essential Question: What types of situations involve addition?

Digital Resources

Solve   Learn   Glossary

Tools   Assessment   Help   Games

Math and Science Project: Baby Animals

Directions Read the character speech bubbles to students. **Find Out!** Have students explore the difference between animals and non-living things. Say: *Animals can have babies. Non-living things cannot have babies. Talk to friends and relatives about different animals and their babies.*
Journal: Make a Poster Have students make a poster. Have them draw a cat with 5 kittens, circle the mother cat and the kittens to join them into one group, and then tell a joining story about how many cats there are in all.

Topic 6

two hundred eighty-one   281

Name _____

Review What You Know

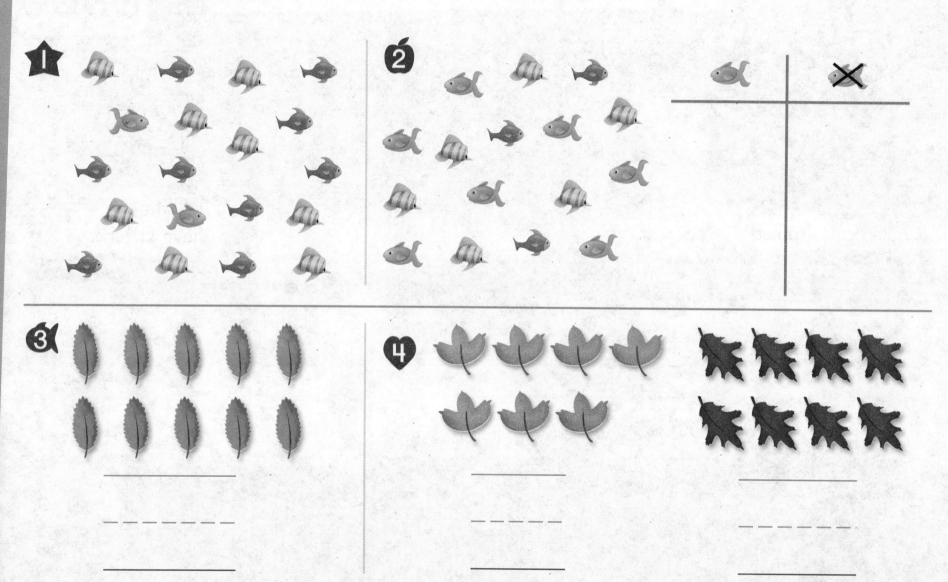

Directions Have students: ⭐ draw a circle around the fish that are purple, and then mark an X on the fish that are NOT purple; 🍎 draw lines in the chart as they count the fish that are blue and the fish that are NOT blue. Then have them draw a circle around the picture at the top of the chart of the group that is greater than the other; ❸ count the leaves, and then write the number to tell how many; ❹ count the leaves, write the numbers to tell how many, and then draw a circle around the number that is less than the other number.

Topic 6

My Word Cards

Directions Have students cut out the vocabulary cards. Read the front of the card, and then ask them to explain what the word or phrase means.

A-Z Glossary

join

in all

addition sentence

add

plus sign (+)

equal sign (=)

My Word Cards

Directions Review the definitions and have students study the cards. Extend learning by having students draw pictures for each word on a separate piece of paper.

3 and 5 is 8.

Point to the addition sentence.
Say: *3 and 5 is 8 is an **addition sentence**. It tells how many there are in all.*

Point to the blue and red blocks.
Say: *There are 6 blocks **in all**.*

Point to each group of flowers.
Say: ***Join** the groups together to find how many flowers there are in all.*

$4 + 3 = 7$

Point to the equal sign.
Say: *This is the **equal sign**. It shows that the part on one side is the same amount as the part on the other side.*

$3 + 1 = 4$

Point to the plus sign.
Say: *This is the **plus sign**. It means add.*

$3 + 2 = 5$

Point to the connecting cubes.
Say: *When you **add** 3 blue cubes to 2 green cubes, you have 5 cubes.*

My Word Cards

A-Z Glossary

Directions Have students cut out the vocabulary cards. Read the front of the card, and then ask them to explain what the word or phrase means.

sum	**equation**	

Directions Review the definitions and have students study the cards. Extend learning by having students draw pictures for each word on a separate piece of paper.

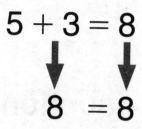

$$5 + 3 = 8$$

$$8 \ = 8$$

Point to one side of the equation at a time.
Say: *An **equation** uses an equal sign to show two sides are the same amount.*

$$2 + 3 = 5$$

Point to the 5.
Say: *The **sum** tells how many in all.*

Solve & Share

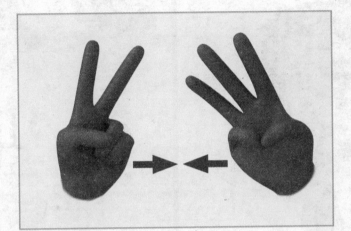

4 🌸 5 🌸 6 🌸

Directions Say: *Carlos holds up 2 flowers in one hand and 3 flowers in another hand. How many flowers does he have in all? Think about the problem in your head. Then act out the story with your fingers to explain. Draw a circle around your answer.*

I can ... show numbers in many ways.

I can also model with math.

Topic 6 | Lesson 1
Digital Resources at SavvasRealize.com
two hundred eighty-seven **287**

☆ Guided Practice

1

2 and 3 is 5 in all.

Directions ⭐ Have students listen to the story, and then do all of the following to show each part to find how many in all: clap and knock, hold up fingers, and give an explanation of a mental image. Ask them to show how many of each color crayon, and then write the number to tell how many in all. *Parker has 2 orange crayons. He has 3 purple crayons. How many crayons does he have in all?*

288 two hundred eighty-eight

Topic 6 | Lesson 1

Name _____

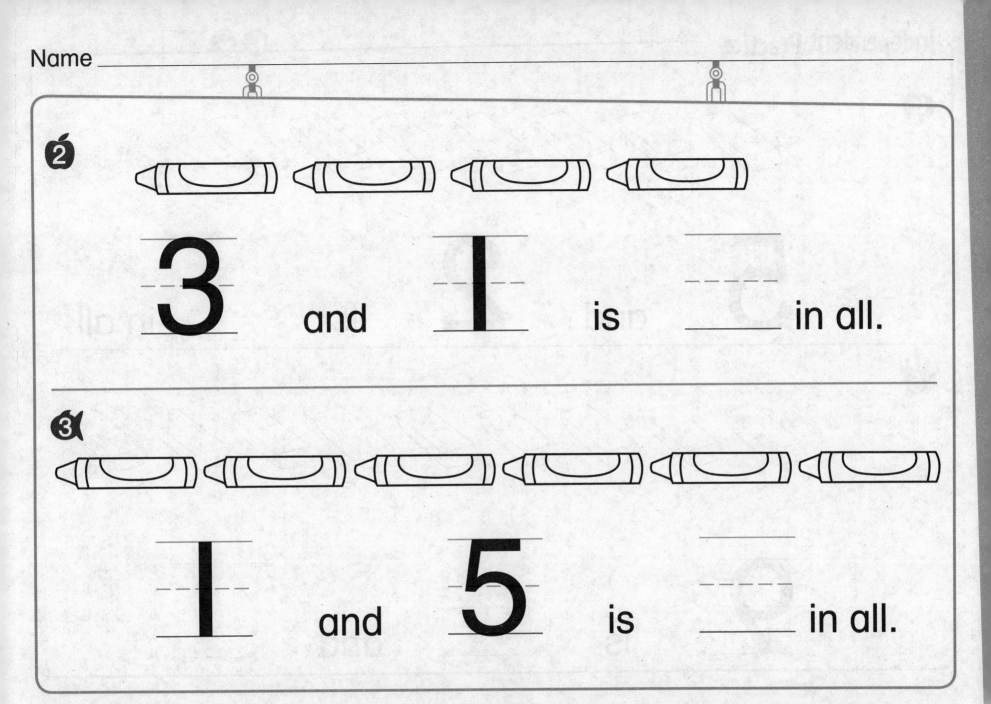

2

3 and I is _____ in all.

3

I and 5 is _____ in all.

Directions Have students listen to the story, and then do all of the following to show each part to find how many in all: clap and knock, hold up fingers, and give an explanation of a mental image. Ask them to color the number of each part, and then write the number to tell how many in all. **2** *Cami has 3 green crayons. She has I blue crayon. How many crayons does she have in all?* **3** *Sammy has I brown crayon. He has 5 purple crayons. How many crayons does he have in all?*

Independent Practice

4

5 and 2 is _____ in all.

✋5

9 is _____ and _____.

Directions **4** Have students listen to the story, and then do all of the following to show each part to find how many in all: clap and knock, hold up fingers, and give an explanation of a mental image. Ask them to color the number of each part, and then write the number to tell how many in all. *Junie has 5 erasers in one pocket. She has 2 erasers in her other pocket. How many erasers does she have in all?* **✋ Higher Order Thinking** Have students listen to the story, color the erasers to show the parts, and then write the numbers to tell how many of each. *Miguel has 9 erasers. He gives some to Aaron. He gives some to Bella. How many does he give to each friend?*

 Topic 6 | Lesson 1

Name _____

Another Look!

2 and **6** is **8** in all.

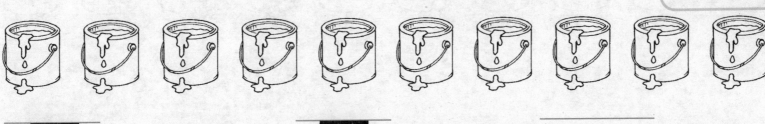

5 and **5** is _____ in all.

Directions Say: *There are 2 yellow paint buckets. There are 6 orange paint buckets. How many paint buckets are there in all?* Model how to clap and knock each part, how to show the parts with fingers, and how to think of the parts with a mental image to find the whole. Then have students color the number of each part, and then write the number to tell how many in all. ⭐ Have students listen to the story, and then do all of the following to show each part to find how many in all: clap and knock, hold up fingers, and give an explanation of a mental image. Ask them to color the number of each part, and then write the number to tell how many in all. *Mattias has 5 red paint buckets. He has 5 blue paint buckets. How many paint buckets does he have in all?*

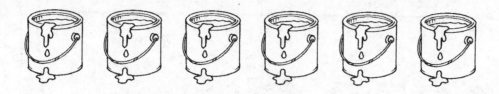

2 and 4 is _____ in all.

10 is _____ and _____ in all.

Directions ❷ Have students listen to the story, and then do all of the following to show each part to find how many in all: clap and knock, hold up fingers, and give an explanation of a mental image. Ask them to color the number of each part, and then write the number to tell how many in all. *Shruthi has 2 green paint buckets. She has 4 blue paint buckets. How many paint buckets does she have in all?* ❸ **Higher Order Thinking** Have students listen to the story, color the paint buckets to show the parts, and then write the numbers to tell how many of each. *Freddy has 10 paint buckets. He fills some with purple paint. He fills the others with red paint. How many does he fill with each color?*

Solve & Share

Name _____

Solve

_____ _____ _____

_____ and _____ is _____.

Directions Say: Daniel sees 1 boat on the water. Then 4 more boats go out onto the water. How many boats are there in all? Show how you know.

I can ...
represent addition as adding to a number.

I can also use math tools correctly.

I and 2 is 3.

☆ Guided Practice

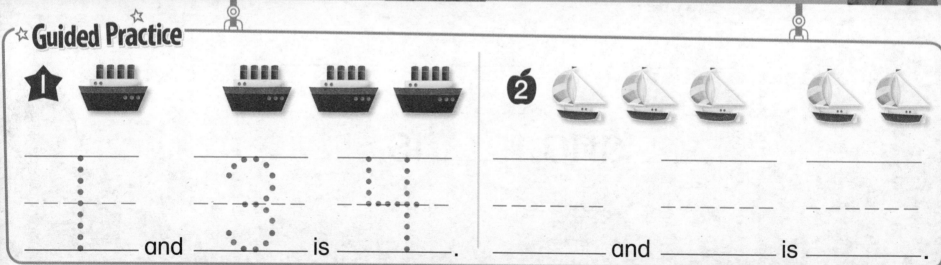

1 _____ and _____ is _____.

2 _____ and _____ is _____.

Directions ⭐ and ② Have students use connecting cubes to model adding to the group when more boats come, and then write an addition sentence to tell how many in all.

Name _____

3

_____ _____

_ _ _ _ _   _ _ _ _ _   _ _ _ _ _

_____ and _____ is _____.

4

_____ _____

_ _ _ _ _   _ _ _ _ _   _ _ _ _ _

_____ and _____ is _____.

5

_____ _____

_ _ _ _ _   _ _ _ _ _   _ _ _ _ _

_____ and _____ is _____.

6

_____ _____

_ _ _ _ _   _ _ _ _ _   _ _ _ _ _

_____ and _____ is _____.

Directions ❸–❻ Have students use connecting cubes to model adding to the group when more boats come, and then write an addition sentence to tell how many in all.

Independent Practice

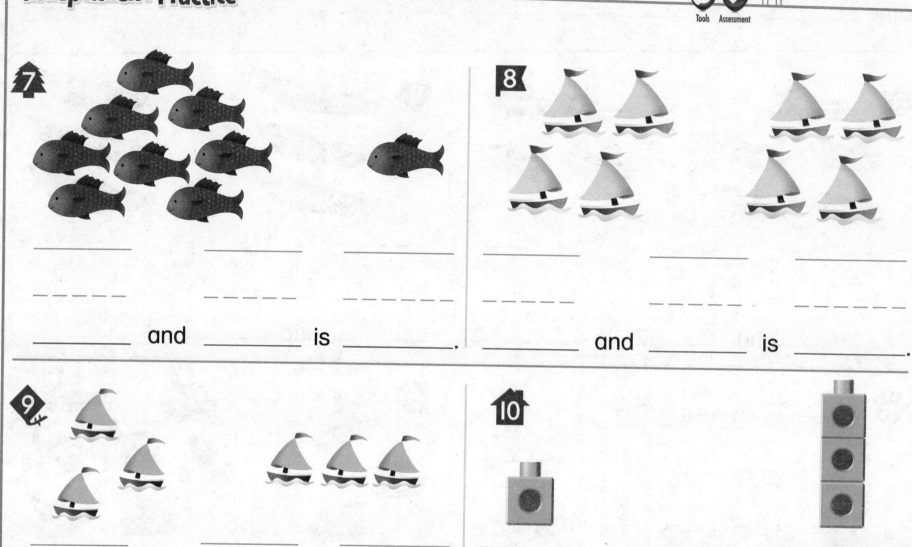

7

_____ _____ is _____ .
and

8

_____ _____ is _____ .
and

9

_____ _____ is _____ .
and

10

_____ _____ is _____ .
and

3

Directions 7–9 Have students use counters to model adding to the group when more fish or boats come, and then write an addition sentence to tell how many in all. **10 Higher Order Thinking** Have students draw the number of green connecting cubes to add to the given connecting cube to make 3 connecting cubes in all, and then complete the addition sentence.

Topic 6 | Lesson 2

Name _____

Another Look!

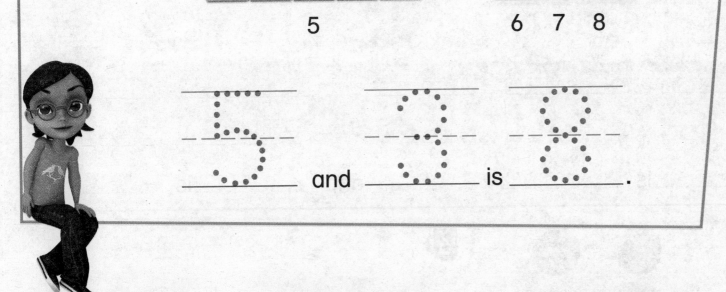

5

6 7 8

5 ____ and ____ 3 ____ is ____ 8 ____.

HOME ACTIVITY Have your child model counting on with paper clips or pennies. For example, ask your child to make a group of 4 paper clips and a group of 3 paper clips. Have your child count the first group, and then from that number, count on the number of paper clips in all.

_____ and _____ is _____ .

_____ and _____ is _____ .

Directions Say: *Marta has some cubes. Then she gets some more. You can write numbers to show how Marta counts on to add more to the group of cubes. Then write an addition sentence to tell how many in all.* ⭐ and ❷ Say: *Daniel has some cubes. Then he gets some more.* Have students count on to add to the group of cubes, and then write an addition sentence to tell how many in all.

Topic 6 | Lesson 2

3

_____ _____

- - - - -   - - - - -

_____ and _____ is _____.

4

_____ _____

- - - - -   - - - - -

_____ and _____ is _____.

5

_____ _____

- - - - -   - - - - -

_____ and _____ is _____.

6

_____ _____

- - - - -   - - - - -

_____ and _____ is _____. **6**

Directions ❸ and ❹ Have students write the numbers to tell how many to add to the group when more boats come, and then write how many there are in all. ✋ **Higher Order Thinking** Have students listen to the story, draw the other group of counters, and then write an addition sentence to match the story. *There are some boats in the water. 6 more boats come. There are 9 boats in all.* ❻ **Higher Order Thinking** Have students draw a group of up to 6 connecting cubes. Then have them draw the number of cubes they need to add to equal 6, and then complete the addition sentence.

     Topic 6 | Lesson 2

 **Solve & Share**

Name _____

Solve

_____   _____   _____

_ _ _ _ _   _ _ _ _ _   _ _ _ _ _
_____   **and**   _____   **is**   _____ .

I can ...
represent addition as putting two or more numbers together.

I can also reason about math.

Directions Say: *Daniel sees 3 tomatoes on a plant. He sees 5 tomatoes on another plant. How many tomatoes are there in all? Show how you know.*

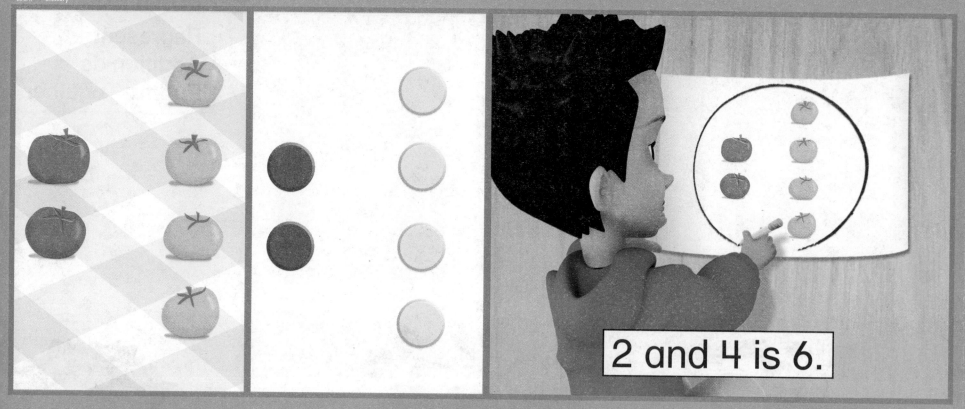

2 and 4 is 6.

☆ Guided Practice

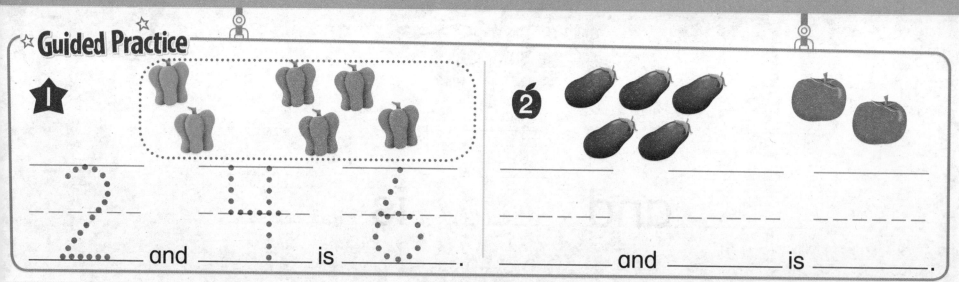

1 ___ and ___ is ___ .

2 ___ and ___ is ___ .

Directions ⭐ and ❷ Have students use counters to model putting together the groups, draw a circle around the groups to put them together, and then write an addition sentence to tell how many in all.

300 three hundred

Topic 6 | Lesson 3

Name _____

3

_____ _____

_____ and _____ is _____ .

4

_____ _____

_____ and _____ is _____ .

5

_____ _____

_____ and _____ is _____ .

6

_____ _____

_____ and _____ is _____ .

Directions ❸ **Vocabulary** Have students draw a circle around the groups to put them together, write an **addition sentence** to tell how many in all, and then say the sentence aloud. ❹–❻ Have students use counters to model putting together the groups, draw a circle around the groups to put them together, and then write an addition sentence to tell how many in all.

Topic 6 | Lesson 3

three hundred one **301**

Independent Practice

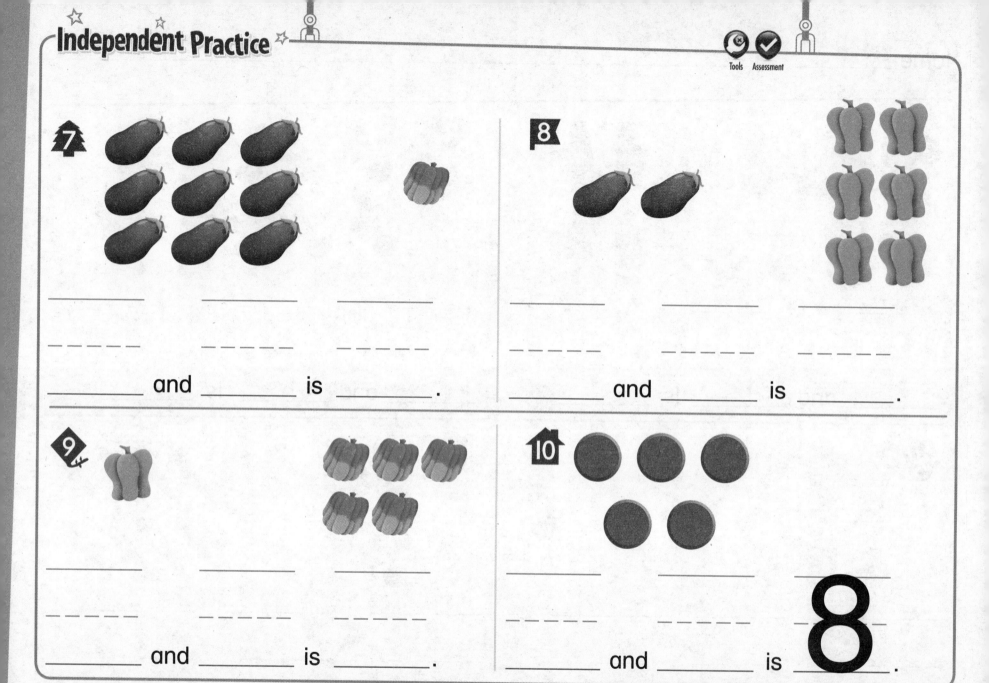

7

_____ _____

_____ and _____ is _____ .

8

_____ _____

_____ and _____ is _____ .

9

_____ _____

_____ and _____ is _____ .

10

_____ _____

_____ and _____ is **8** .

Directions ⭐ **Math and Science** Say: _What do plants need to grow?_ Have students name the vegetables, draw a circle around the groups to put them together, and then write an addition sentence to tell how many in all. **8** and **9** Have students use counters as a model to put together the groups, draw a circle around the groups to put them together, and then write an addition sentence to tell how many in all. **10 Higher Order Thinking** Have students draw the other group of counters, draw a circle around the groups to put them together, and then complete the addition sentence.

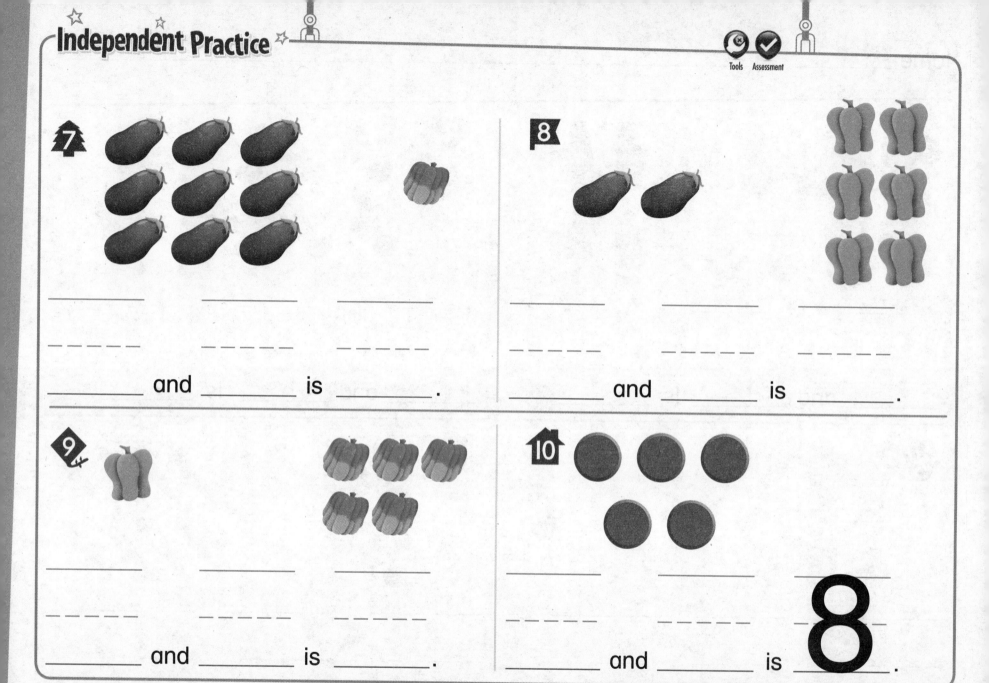

302 three hundred two

Topic 6 | Lesson 3

Name _____

Another Look!

1 and 4 is 5.

HOME ACTIVITY Take turns choosing a problem on this page and making up a number story about it. One person tells the story, and the other person writes the complete addition sentence. For example, 1 and 4 is 5.

⭐
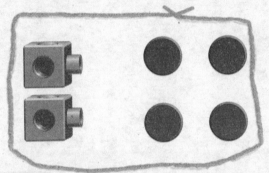

____ and ____ is ____.

🍎
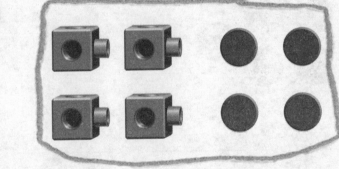

____ and ____ is ____.

Directions Say: *How many cubes are there? How many counters are there? When you put the math tools together with yarn, you can count them all to find how many. Write how many of each math tool there is, and then write an addition sentence to tell how many in all.*
⭐ and 🍎 Have students write the numbers to tell how many of each math tool there is, and then write an addition sentence to tell how many in all.

3

_____ _____ _____

_____ and _____ is _____ .

4

_____ _____ _____

_____ and _____ is _____ .

5

_____ _____ _____

_____ and _____ is 9 .

6

_____ _____ _____

_____ and _____ is 7 .

Directions **3** and **4** Have students put together the math tools, draw a circle around the groups to put them together, and then write an addition sentence to tell how many in all. **5** **Higher Order Thinking** Have students draw the other group, draw a circle around the groups to put them together, and then complete the addition sentence. **6** **Higher Order Thinking** Have students draw counters to show two groups that equal 7 when put together, and then complete the addition sentence.

304 three hundred four

Topic 6 | Lesson 3

Solve & Share

Name _____

Solve

I can ...
add numbers together.

I can also reason about math.

Directions Say: *There are 4 crayons in a box. Daniel puts 3 red crayons in the box. How can you find how many crayons there are in all?*

Digital Resources at SavvasRealize.com

4 and 2

☆ Guided Practice

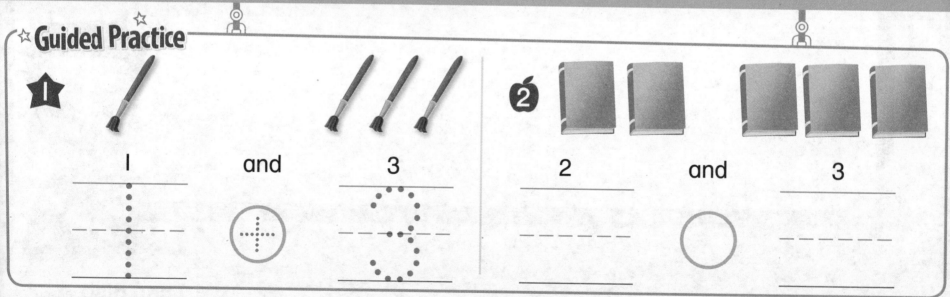

1 1 and 3

2 2 and 3

Directions ⬆ and ❷ Have students count the school supplies in each group, and then write the numbers and the plus sign to show adding the groups.

Topic 6 | Lesson 4

3 3 and 4

‒ ‒ ‒ ‒ ‒ ‒ ◯ ‒ ‒ ‒ ‒ ‒ ‒

4 5 and 1

‒ ‒ ‒ ‒ ‒ ‒ ◯ ‒ ‒ ‒ ‒ ‒ ‒

5 3 and 3

‒ ‒ ‒ ‒ ‒ ‒ ◯ ‒ ‒ ‒ ‒ ‒ ‒

6 2 and 1

‒ ‒ ‒ ‒ ‒ ‒ ◯ ‒ ‒ ‒ ‒ ‒ ‒

Directions ❸–✋ Have students count the school supplies in each group, and then write the numbers and the plus sign to show adding the groups. **6 Number Sense** Have students count all the bookmarks, write the numbers and the plus sign to show adding, and then explain how counting forward relates to adding.

Topic 6 | Lesson 4

three hundred seven **307**

Independent Practice

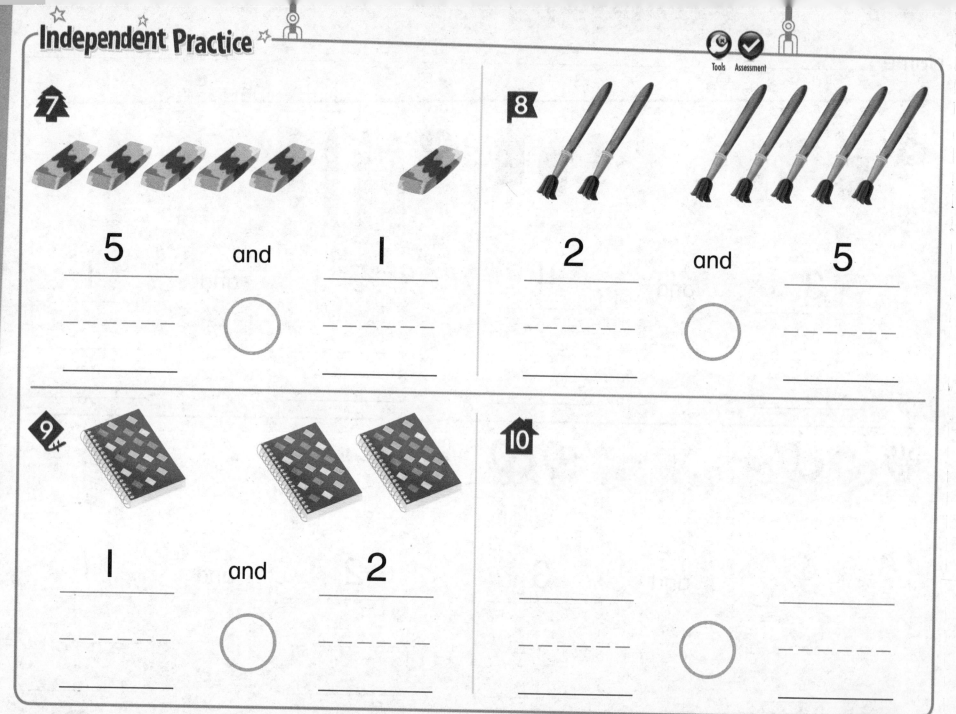

7

5   and   I

◯

8

2   and   5

◯

9

I   and   2

◯

10

◯

Directions 7—9 Have students count the school supplies in each group, and then write the numbers and the plus sign to show adding the groups. **10 Higher Order Thinking** Have students draw two groups of counters to show 5 in all, and then write the number of counters in each group and the plus sign to show adding the groups.

Topic 6 | Lesson 4

Name _____

Help Tools Games

Homework & Practice 6-4

Use the Plus Sign

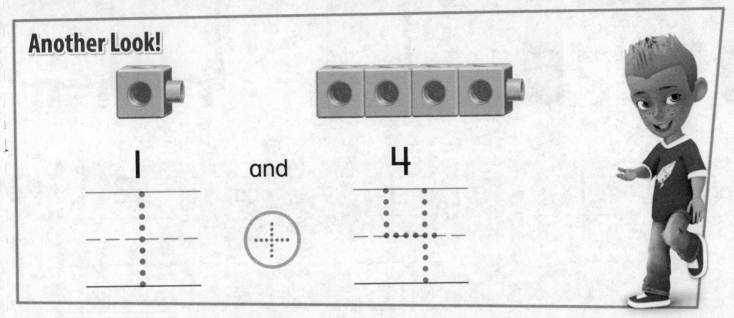

Another Look!

1 and 4

HOME ACTIVITY Show your child two groups of pennies and have your child write an addition expression with a plus sign to show adding the groups. For example, show a group of 2 pennies and a group of 5 pennies. Help your child write the addition expression 2 + 5.

4 and 2

   and

2 and 3

Directions Say: *You can use connecting cubes or other objects to add* 1 *and* 4. *Write the numbers and the plus sign to show how to add the groups.* ⭐ *and* ❷ *Have students count the objects in each group, and then write the numbers and the plus sign to show adding the groups.*

Topic 6 | Lesson 4   Digital Resources at SavvasRealize.com   three hundred nine **309**

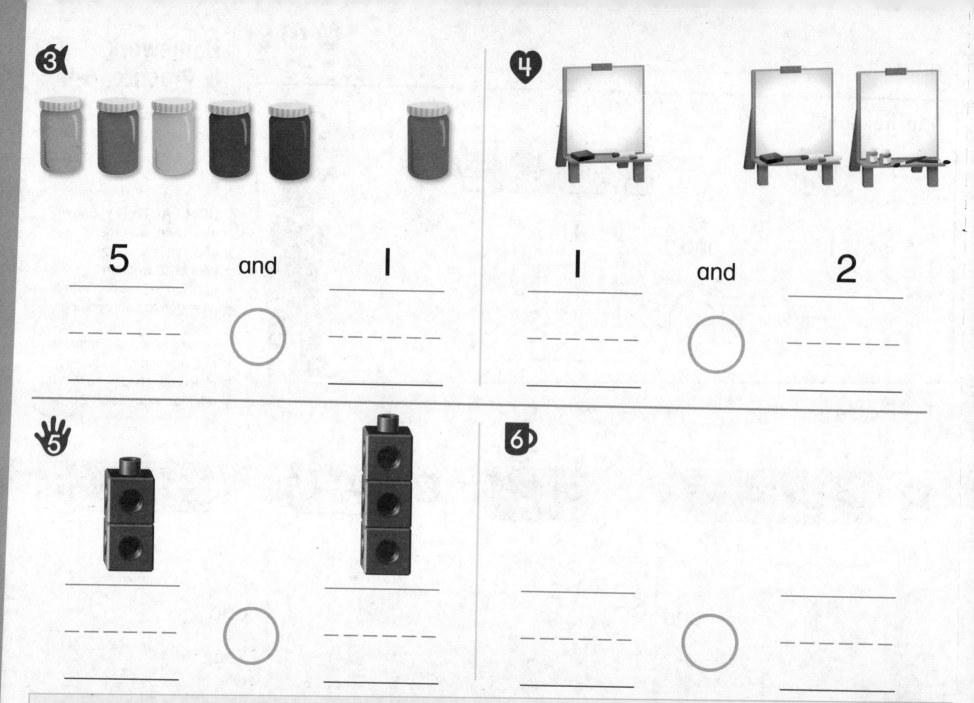

3

5 and 1

_____ ◯ _ _ _ _

4

1 and 2

_ _ _ _ _ ◯ _ _ _ _

5

_ _ _ _ _ ◯ _ _ _ _

6

_ _ _ _ _ ◯ _ _ _ _

Directions ❸ and ❹ Have students count the art supplies in each group, and then write the numbers and the plus sign to show adding the groups. ✋ **Higher Order Thinking** Have students count the connecting cubes in each group, and then write the numbers and the plus sign to show adding the groups. ❻ **Higher Order Thinking** Have students draw two groups of apples that equal 6 apples in all when added together, and then write the number of apples in each group and the plus sign to show adding the groups.

310 three hundred ten

Topic 6 | Lesson 4

Name _____

Lesson 6-5

Represent and Explain Addition with Equations

Directions Say: *Daniel counts 4 drums in a parade. Then he sees 1 more drum. What numbers do you add to find how many drums he sees in all? How can you show the adding?*

I can ...
write an equation to show addition.

I can also reason about math.

Digital Resources at SavvasRealize.com

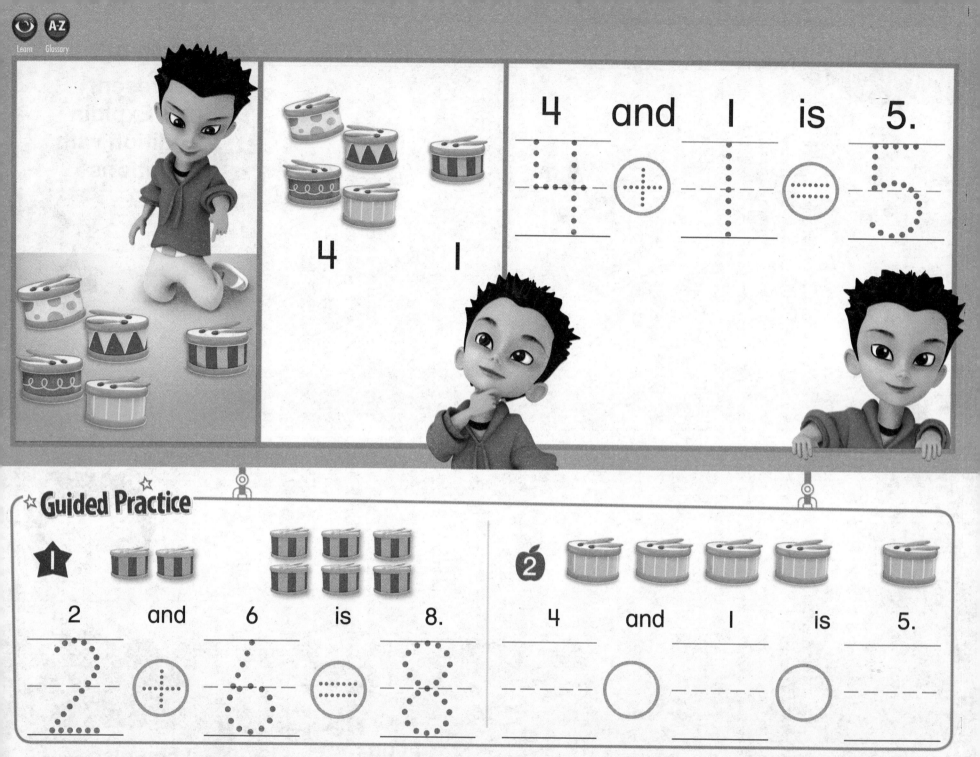

4 and 1 is 5.

4 $+$ 1 $=$ 5

☆ **Guided Practice**

⭐ 1

2 and 6 is 8.

2 $+$ 6 $=$ 8

2

4 and 1 is 5.

____ ◯ ____ ◯ ____

Directions ⭐ and ② Have students add the groups to find the sum, and then write an equation to show the addition.

312 three hundred twelve

Name _____

3

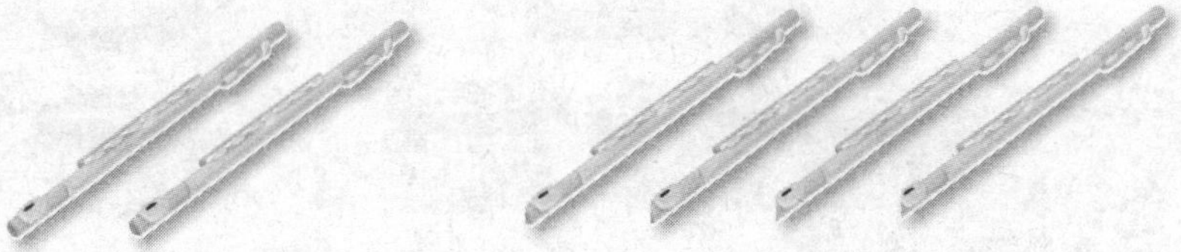

2 and 4 is 6.

◯ ◯

_____

4

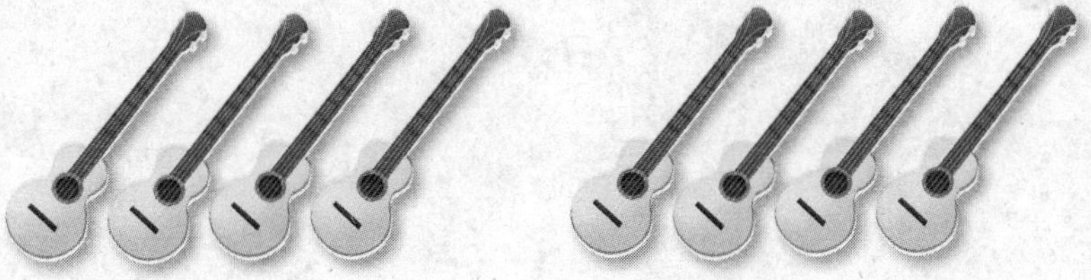

4 and 4 is 8.

◯ ◯

_____

5

6 and 1 is 7.

◯ ◯

_____

6

3 and 4 is 7.

◯ ◯

_____

Directions **3–6** Have students add the groups to find the sum, and then write an equation to show the addition.

Topic 6 | Lesson 5

three hundred thirteen **313**

Independent Practice

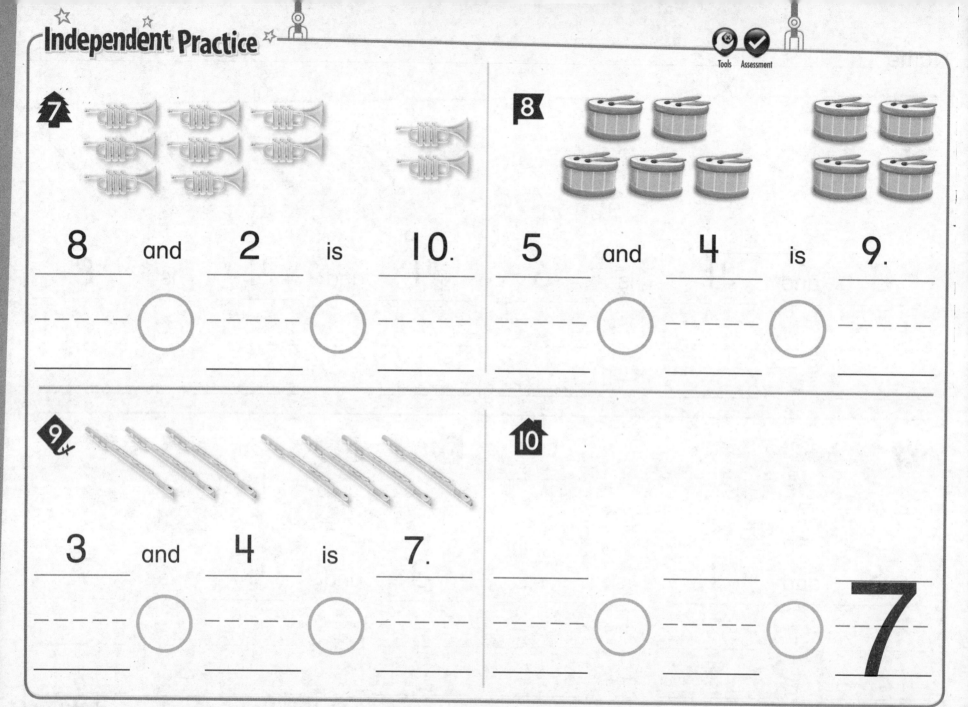

7

8 and 2 is 10.

◯ ◯

8

5 and 4 is 9.

◯ ◯

9

3 and 4 is 7.

◯ ◯

10

◯ ◯

7

Name _____

Help Tools Games

Homework & Practice 6-5

Represent and Explain Addition with Equations

Another Look!

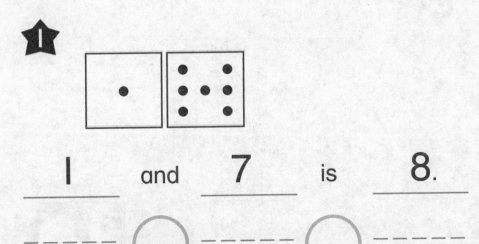

4 and 5 is 9.

HOME ACTIVITY Make a set of number cards from 1 to 5. Shuffle them and place them facedown on a table. Take turns picking 2 number cards and finding the sum of the two numbers. Work with your child to write a number sentence using the plus and equal signs.

1

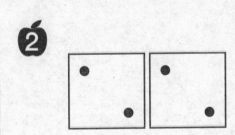

1 and 7 is 8.

_____ ◯ _____ ◯ _____

2

2 and 2 is 4.

_____ ◯ _____ ◯ _____

Directions Say: *What numbers do the dot cards show? Write the numbers, the plus sign, the equal sign, and the sum to show addition.* 1 and 2 Have students add the groups to find the sum, and then write an equation to show the addition.

Topic 6 | Lesson 5   Digital Resources at SavvasRealize.com   three hundred fifteen **315**

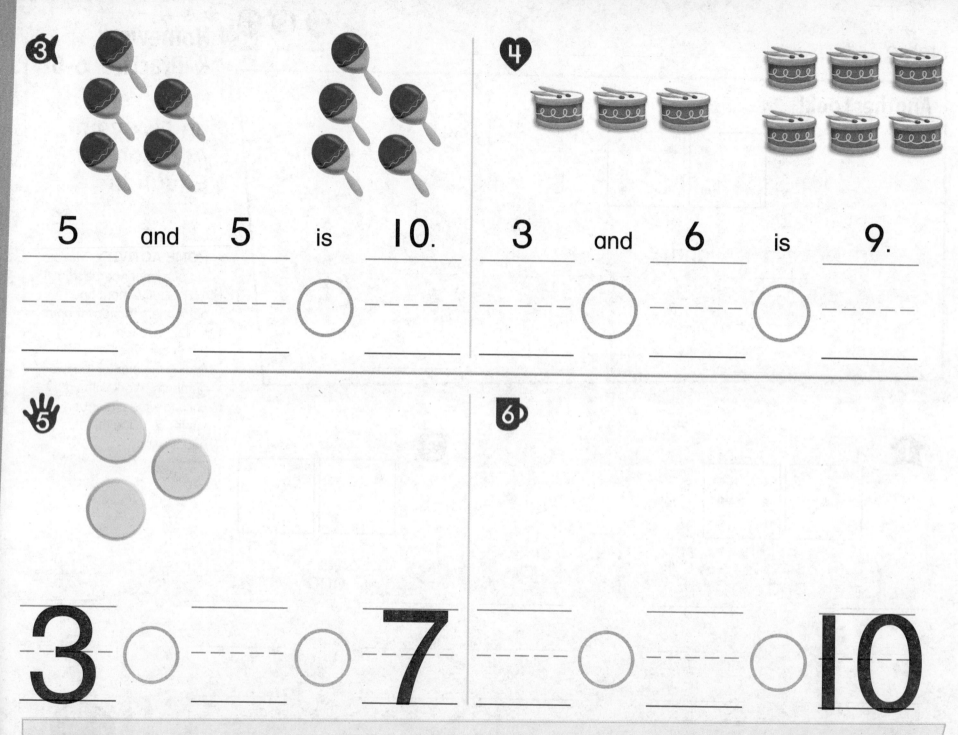

3

5   and   5   is   10.

___ ◯ ___ ◯ ___

4

3   and   6   is   9.

___ ◯ ___ ◯ ___

5

3 ◯ ___ ◯ 7

6

___ ◯ ___ ◯ 10

Directions **3** and **4** Have students add the groups to find the sum, and then write an equation to show the addition. **5 Algebra** Have students draw the other group, add the groups to find the sum, and then complete the equation. **6 Higher Order Thinking** Have students draw counters to show two groups that add up to 10, and then complete the equation.

316 three hundred sixteen

Name _____

Solve

Lesson 6-6
Continue to
Represent
and Explain
Addition with
Equations

‒ ‒ ‒ ‒ ◯ ‒ ‒ ‒ ‒ ◯ ‒ ‒ ‒

Directions Say: *Daniel sees 2 rabbits under a bush. He sees 5 other rabbits eating grass. How many rabbits are there in all? What equation can you write to solve the problem?*

I can ...
use the plus sign and equal sign in an equation.

I can also use math tools correctly.

Digital Resources at SavvasRealize.com

3
  3

$3 + 3 = 6$

2   2

$2 + 2 = 4$

☆ **Guided Practice**

1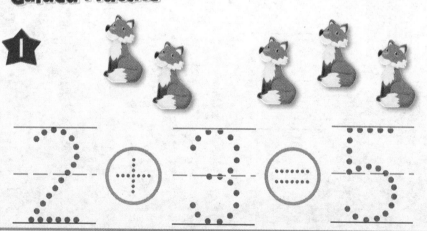

2 ⊕ 5

2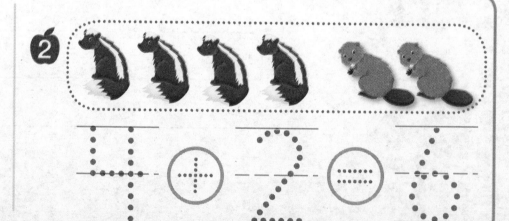

4 ⊕ 2 ⊕ 6

Directions ⭐ Have students add one group of foxes to the other, and then write an equation to show the addition. 🍎 Have students put together the groups of animals, and then write an equation to show the addition.

318 three hundred eighteen

Topic 6 | Lesson 6

Name _____

3

_____ _____
◯ ◯
- - - - - - - - -

♥ 4

_____ _____
◯ ◯
- - - - - - - - -

✋ 5

_____ _____
◯ ◯
- - - - - - - - -

6

_____ _____
◯ ◯
- - - - - - - - -

Directions ③ and ④ Have students put together the groups of animals, and then write an equation to show the addition.
✋ and ⑥ Have students add one group of animals to the other, and then write an equation to show the addition.

Independent Practice

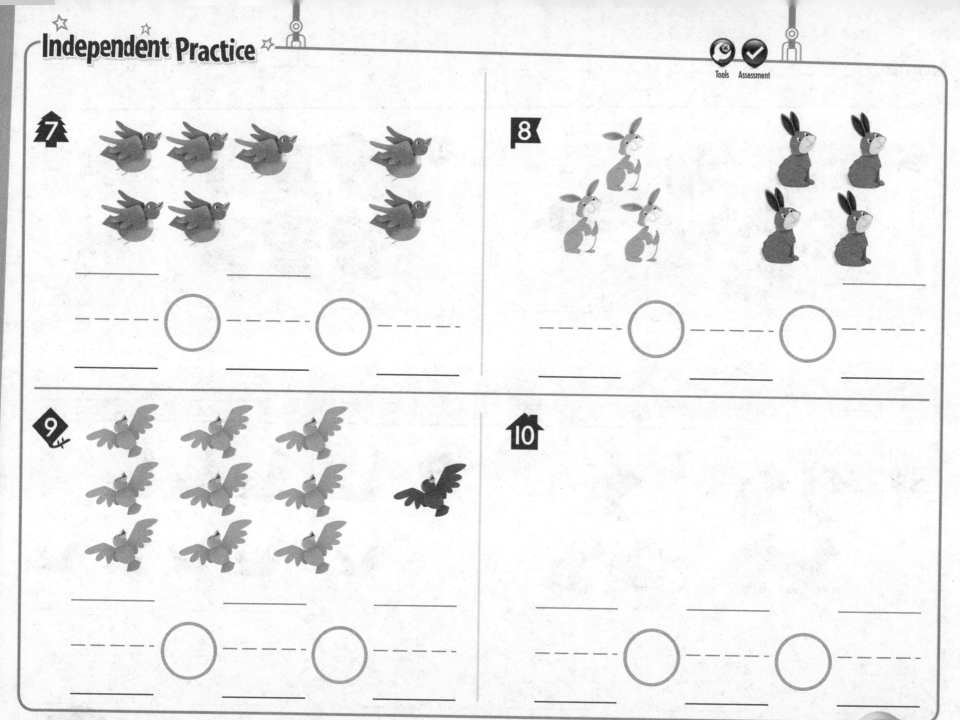

7

8

9

10

Directions **7** and **8** Have students add one group of birds to the other, and then write an equation to show the addition. **9** Have students put together the groups of animals, and then write an equation to show the addition. **10** **Higher Order Thinking** Have students draw counters to show two groups that add up to 9, and then write an equation to show the addition.

Topic 6 | Lesson 6

Name _____

Help   Tools   Games

Homework & Practice 6-6

Continue to Represent and Explain Addition with Equations

Another Look!

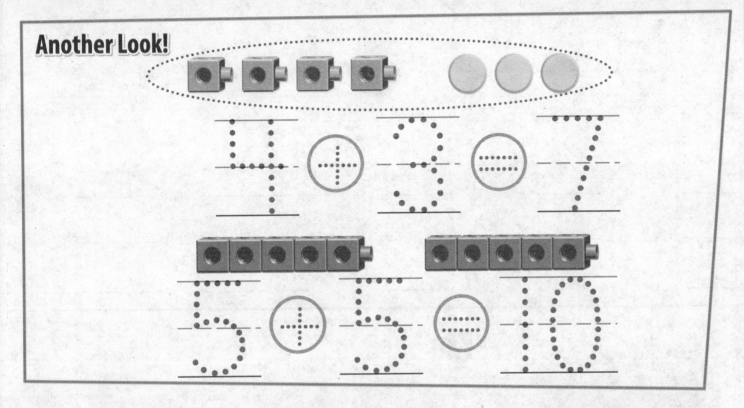

$4 + 3 = 7$

$5 + 5 = 10$

HOME ACTIVITY Make two groups of pennies and have your child write an equation that shows joining the groups together. For example, show a group of 5 pennies and a group of 4 pennies, and help your child write $5 + 4 = 9$.

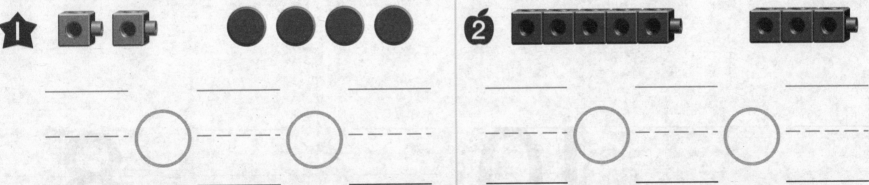

Directions Say: *Make a group of 4 connecting cubes or other objects, and a group of 3 counters or other objects. Now put the groups together to find out how many there are in all. Write the numbers, plus sign, equal sign, and sum to make the equation that shows the addition. Now make a group of 5 connecting cubes or other objects, and another group of 5 connecting cubes or other objects. Add one group to the other to find how many there are in all. Write an equation to show the addition.* ★ Have students put together the groups of math tools, and then write an equation to show the addition. ② Have students add one group of math tools to the other, and then write an equation to show the addition.

Topic 6 | Lesson 6   Digital Resources at SavvasRealize.com   three hundred twenty-one **321**

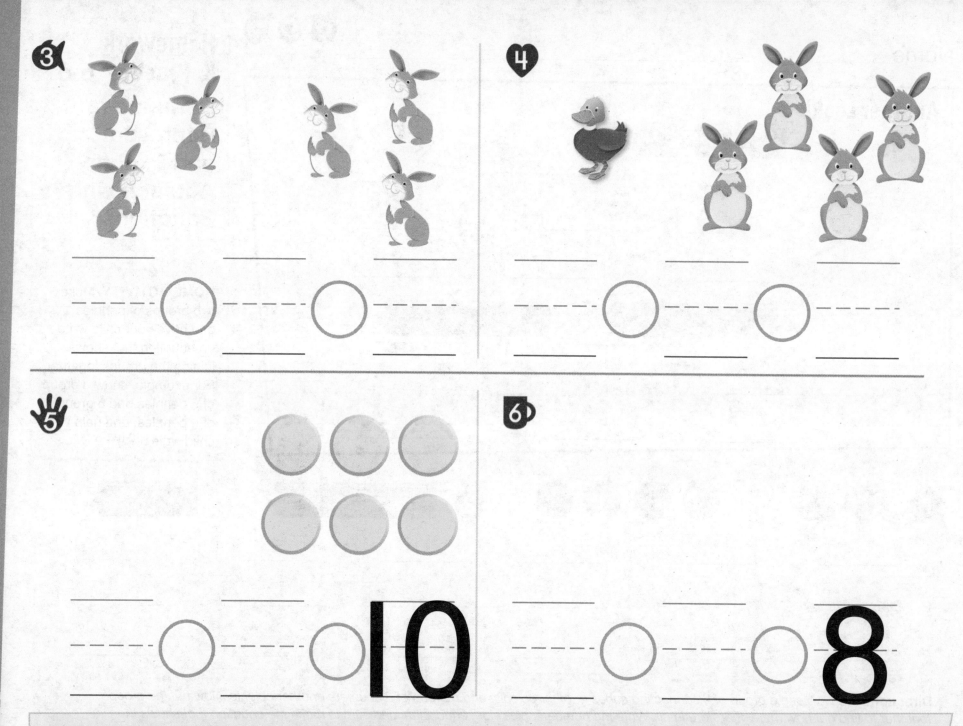

3

_____ ◯ _____ ◯ _____

4

_____ ◯ _____ ◯ _____

5

_____ ◯ _____ ◯ |0

6

_____ ◯ _____ ◯ 8

Directions ❸ Have students add one group of rabbits to the other, and then write an equation to show the addition. ❹ Have students put together the groups of animals, and then write an equation to show the addition. ✋ **Higher Order Thinking** Have students draw the other group, add to or put the groups together, and then complete the equation to show addition. ❻ **Higher Order Thinking** Have students draw counters to show two groups that add up to 8, and then complete the equation to show addition.

Solve & Share

Name _____

Solve

Lesson 6-7
Solve Addition
Word Problems:
Add To

Directions Say: *4 squirrels are eating lunch at the squirrel feeder. 2 more join them. How many are eating at the feeder now? Show how you know in two ways, and then explain how you know.*

I can ... solve addition problems.

I can also model with math.

6 + 3 = 9

☆ **Guided Practice**

1

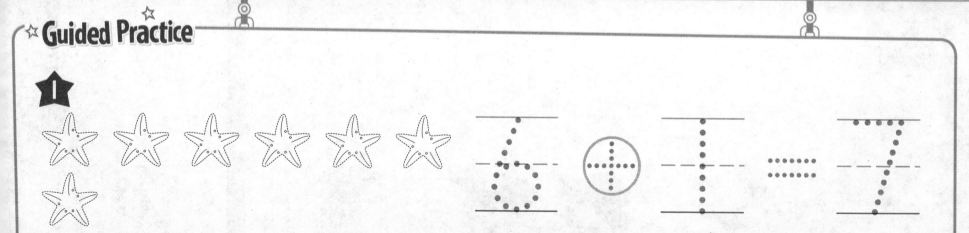

Directions Have students listen to the story, draw a picture to show what is happening, and then write the equation. Then have them explain their work. ★ *There are 6 sea stars on the beach. 1 more joins them. How many sea stars are there in all?*

Topic 6 | Lesson 7

🍎 **2**

🦀 **3**

❤️ **4**

✋ **5**

Directions Have students listen to the story, use counters to show the addition, draw a picture, and then write an equation to tell how many in all. **🍎2** *3 crabs sit on the beach. 7 more join them. How many crabs are sitting in all?* **🦀3** *5 crabs look for food. 4 more join them. How many crabs are there in all?* **❤️4** *There is 1 turtle on the beach. 5 more walk up. How many turtles are there in all?* **✋5** *2 turtles swim in the water. 6 more join them. How many turtles are swimming in all?*

Topic 6 | Lesson 7   three hundred twenty-five **325**

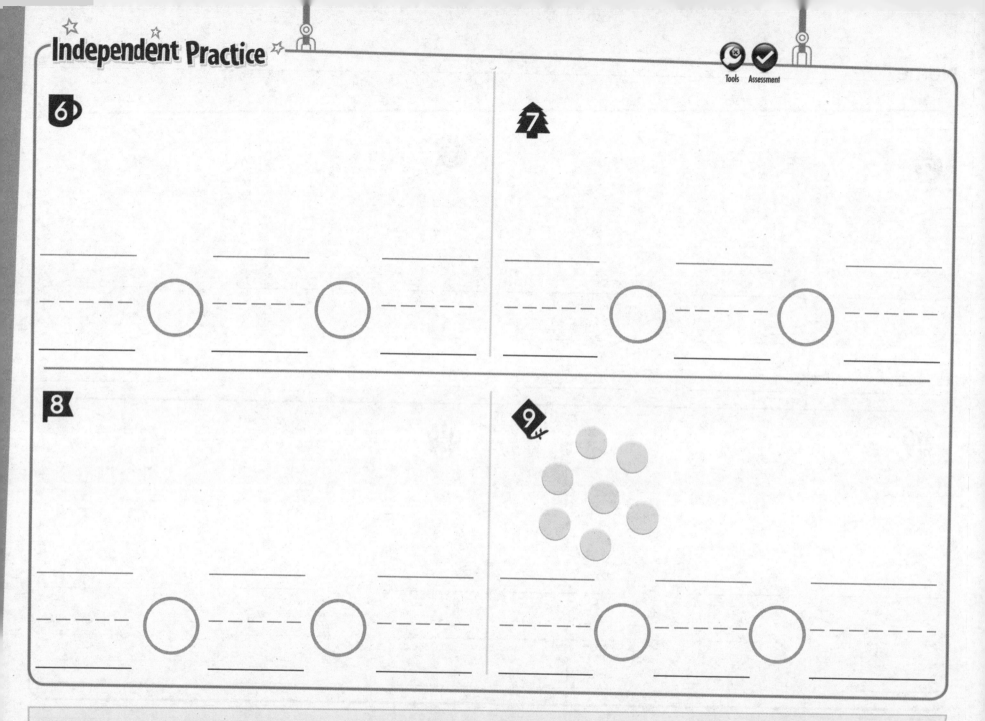

6

7

8

9

Directions Have students listen to the story, use counters to show the addition, draw a picture, and then write an equation to tell how many in all. **6** *4 girls play at the beach. 4 boys join them. How many children are there in all?* **7** *8 children rest on the sand. I girl joins them. How many children are there in all?* **8** *2 boys play in the water. 5 girls join them. How many children are there in all?* **9 Higher Order Thinking** Have students listen to the story, draw counters to complete the picture, and write an equation. *7 children build a sand castle. Some more help them. There are 10 children building in all. How many more come to help them?*

Name _____

Another Look!

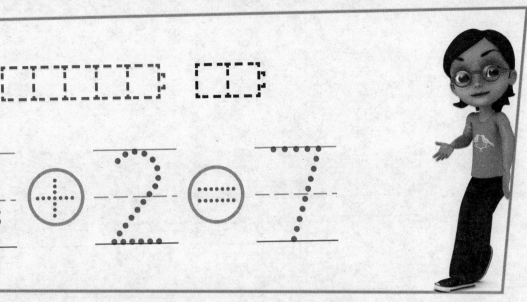

HOME ACTIVITY Give your child two numbers up to 10. Ask him or her to tell an addition story using the numbers. Repeat with different numbers.

⭐ 1

🍎 2

Directions Say: *How can you explain the equation* 5 + 2 = 7 *?* Guide students to tell an addition story using the equation. Have students listen to the story, use connecting cubes to show the addition, draw a picture, and write an equation. ⭐ *4 fish swim in the water. 6 more join them. How many fish are there in all?* 🍎 *2 sea stars lie on a rock. 3 more join them. How many sea stars are there in all?*

3

 4

 5

$$8 + 2 = 10$$

6

Directions Have students listen to the story, use a model to show the addition, draw a picture, and write an equation. **3** *4 flowers grow in a pond. 3 more grow. How many flowers are there in all?* **4** *2 butterflies sit on a bush. 6 more join them. How many butterflies are there in all?* **5 Higher Order Thinking** Have students tell an addition story that matches the equation, and then draw a picture to show what is happening. **6 Higher Order Thinking** Have students tell an addition story that matches the picture, and then write an equation to match.

Solve & Share

Name _____

Directions Say: *Daniel's teacher is making name tags for her students. She makes 3 name tags for boys. She makes 2 more for girls. Now she has 5 name tags. How does Daniel's teacher know that she has made 5 name tags? Explain and then show how you know.*

I can ...
use equations to represent and explain addition.

I can also make math arguments.

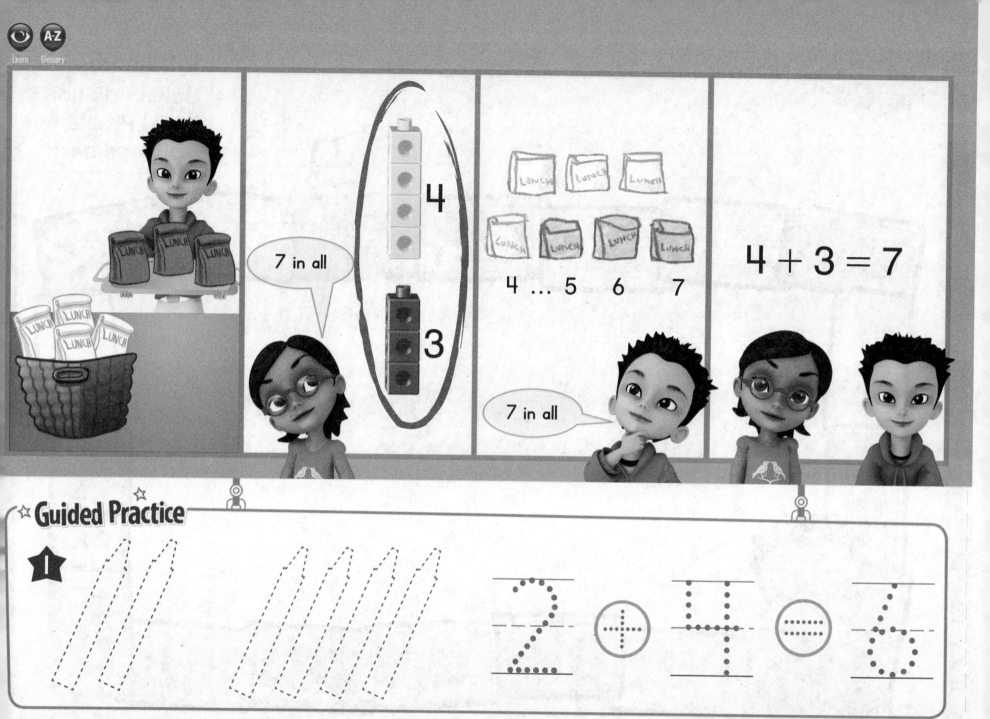

☆ Guided Practice

1

2 ⊕ 4 ⊜ 6

Directions ⭐ Have students listen to the story, draw a picture to show what is happening, and then write an equation. Then have them explain their work. *Daniel puts 2 red crayons and 4 blue crayons on the table. Now there are 6 crayons in all. How can Daniel tell there are 6 crayons?*

Topic 6 | Lesson 8

🍎 **2**

🐢 **3**

❤️ **4**

✋ **5**

Directions Have students listen to each story, draw a picture to show what is happening, and then write an equation. Then have them explain their work. 🍎 *Jorge puts 4 blue paint jars and 3 red paint jars in the art room. How many paint jars are there in all?* 🐢 *Maya has 3 green pencils and 2 orange pencils. How many pencils are there in all?* ❤️ *Rex has 1 sheet of blue paper and 8 sheets of yellow paper. How many sheets of paper does he have in all?* ✋ *Reagan has 4 green blocks and 4 yellow blocks. How many blocks does she have in all?*

Independent Practice

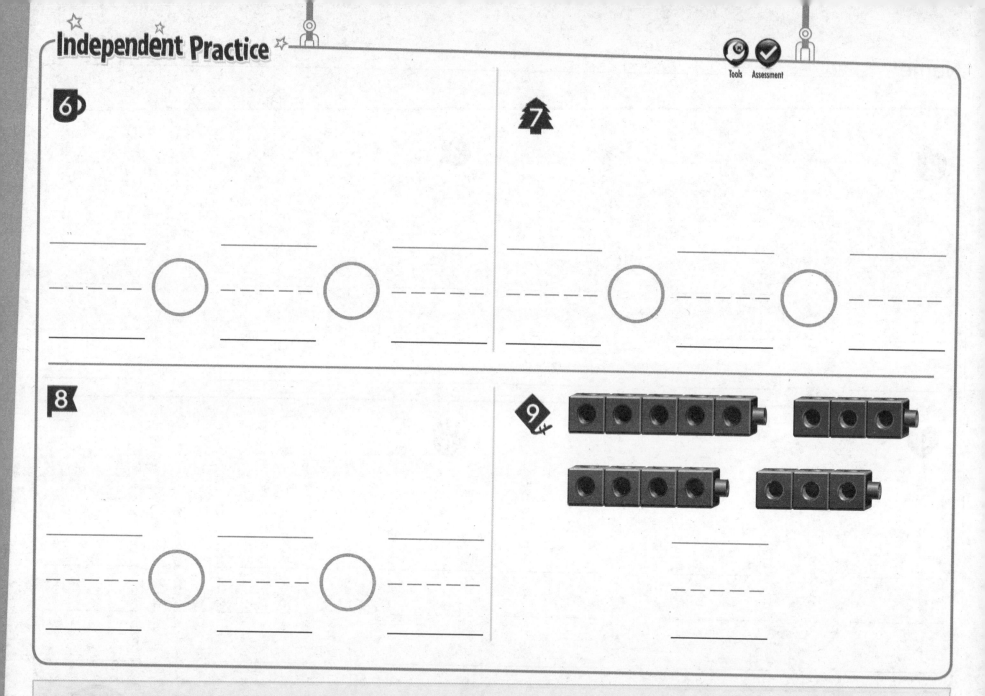

6

7

8

9

Directions Have students listen to each story, draw a picture to show what is happening, and then write an equation. **6** *Benny puts 5 bananas in a bowl and 4 bananas on a plate. How many bananas does he have in all?* **7** *Kris eats 2 grapes at lunch and 6 grapes for her snack. How many grapes does she eat in all?* **8** *There are 4 girls and 2 boys on a train ride. How many children ride the train in all?* **9 Higher Order Thinking** Have students listen to the story, circle the connecting cubes that show the story and tell why the other cubes do not show the story, and then write the number to tell how many in all. Say: *Jimmy picks 5 raspberries. Then he picks 3 more. How many raspberries does he have in all?*

Name _____

Help Tools Games

Homework & Practice 6-8
Solve Addition Word Problems: Put Together

Another Look!

5 + 3 = 8

 1

 2

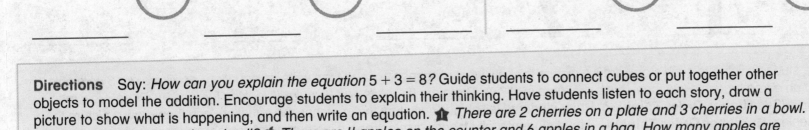

Directions Say: *How can you explain the equation* 5 + 3 = 8? Guide students to connect cubes or put together other objects to model the addition. Encourage students to explain their thinking. Have students listen to each story, draw a picture to show what is happening, and then write an equation. 🟊 *There are 2 cherries on a plate and 3 cherries in a bowl. How many cherries are there in all?* 🍎 *There are 4 apples on the counter and 6 apples in a bag. How many apples are there in all?*

HOME ACTIVITY Give your child a group of 2 pennies and a group of 3 pennies and ask: *How can you tell there are 5 coins in all?* Encourage your child to show how he or she knows by lining up the coins and using words to describe how to add the groups together.

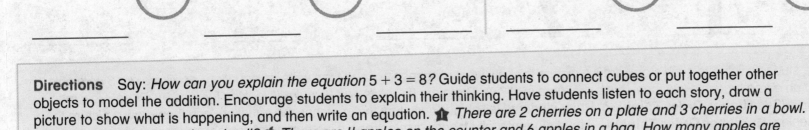

3

◯ ◯

4

◯ ◯

5

$$6 + 1 = 7$$

6

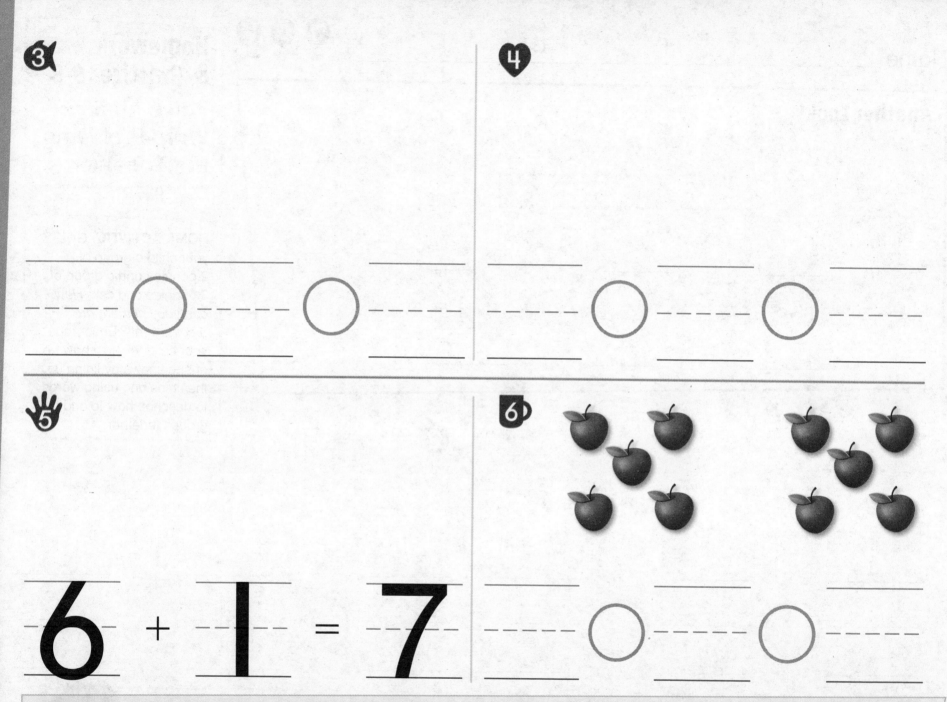

◯ ◯

_____   _____   _____

\- - - - -   +   \- - - - -   =   \- - - - -

_____   _____   _____

\- - - - -   +   \- - - - -   =   \- - - - -

_____   _____   _____

_____   _____   _____

\- - - - -   +   \- - - - -   =   \- - - - -

_____   _____   _____

Directions Say: *Use blue and red cubes to make stacks of 2 cubes. How many different ways can you make a stack of 2 cubes? Write equations to describe your stacks. Use a blue crayon to tell how many blue cubes and a red crayon to tell how many red cubes.*

I can ... use patterns to add numbers together.

I can also look for patterns.

Topic 6 | Lesson 9
Digital Resources at SavvasRealize.com
three hundred thirty-five **335**

$$5 + 0 = 5$$
$$4 + 1 = 5$$
$$3 + 2 = 5$$
$$2 + 3 = 5$$
$$1 + 4 = 5$$
$$0 + 5 = 5$$

$$5 + 0 = 5$$
$$0 + 5 = 5$$

$$1 + 4 = 5$$
$$4 + 1 = 5$$

$$3 + 2 = 5$$
$$2 + 3 = 5$$

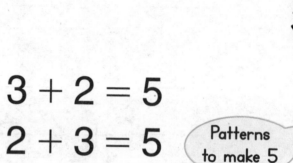

Patterns to make 5

☆ **Guided Practice**

1

    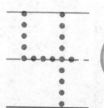   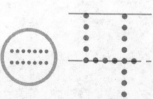

Directions ⭐ Have students color a way to make 4, and then write an equation to match the boxes.

Name _____

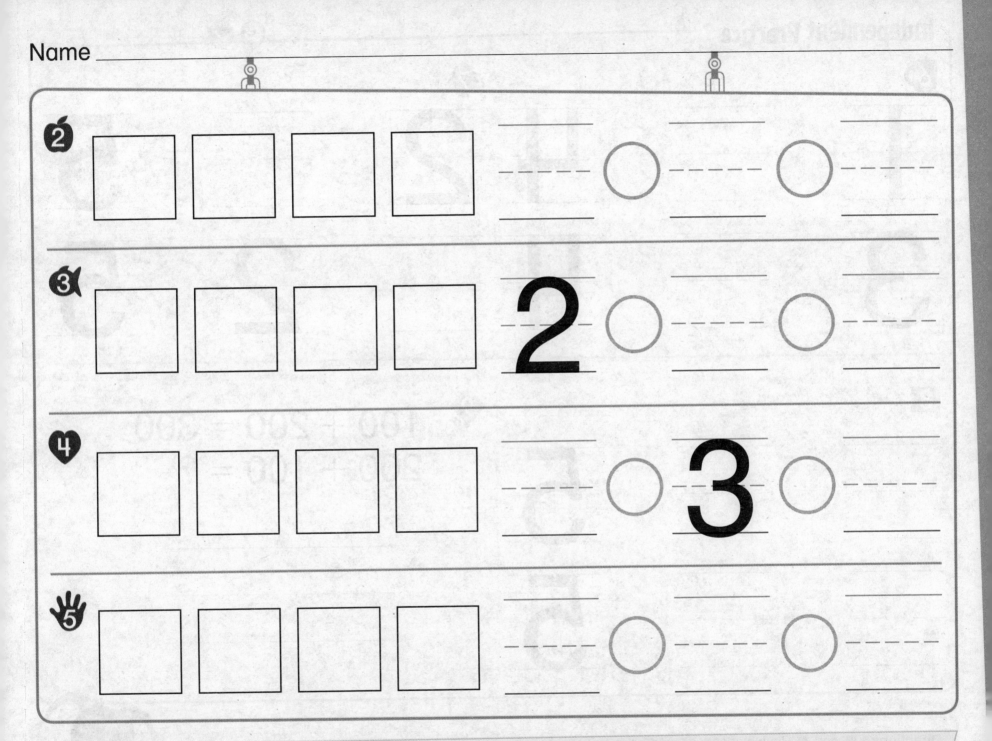

Directions 🍎–✋ Have students color the boxes to complete the pattern started on the page before of ways to make 4, and then write an equation to match the boxes.

6 1 ◯ ___ ◯ 4

3 ◯ ___ ◯ 4

7 2 ◯ ___ ◯ 5

4 ◯ 2 ◯ 5

8

___ ◯ ___ ◯ 5

___ ◯ ___ ◯ 5

9

$$100 + 200 = 300$$
$$200 + 100 = ?$$

_____

_____

Name _____

Help   Tools   Games

Another Look!

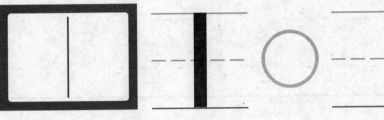

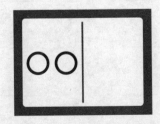

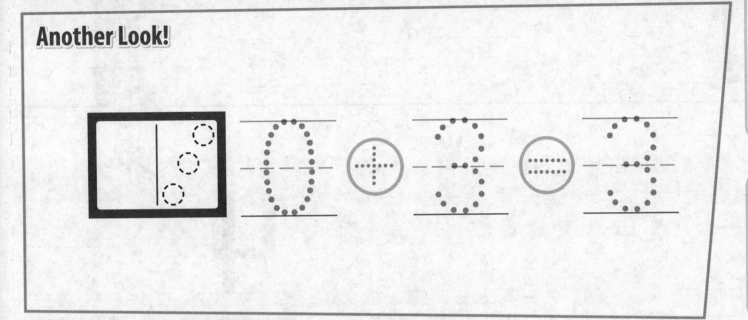

Homework & Practice 6-9

Use Patterns to Develop Fluency in Addition

HOME ACTIVITY Give your child an equation with sums up to 5. Ask him or her to write the matching pair. For example, write *1 + 3 = 4.* Your child should write *3 + 1 = 4.*

Directions Say: *Draw counters to show how to make 3. Write an equation to match the counters.* ★ and ❷ Have students draw counters to complete the pattern of ways to make 3, and then write an equation to match the counters.

Topic 6 | Lesson 9   Digital Resources at SavvasRealize.com   three hundred thirty-nine **339**

3

4

3

5

4

6

Topic 6 | Lesson 9

Name _____

Think.

_____   _____   _____

-----   **+**   -----   **=**   -----

_____   _____   _____

Directions Say: *Daniel sees a group of 3 fluffy, white clouds in the sky. Marta sees 1 gray cloud. How many clouds do they see in all? Draw a picture to show what is happening, and then write the equation to tell how many clouds in all. Explain how you know.*

I can ...
model adding different numbers together by drawing, counting, or writing equations.

I can also find correct sums.

3 + 3

3 + 3 = 6

6 fish

How can I show it?

Draw.

Count.

☆ Guided Practice

1

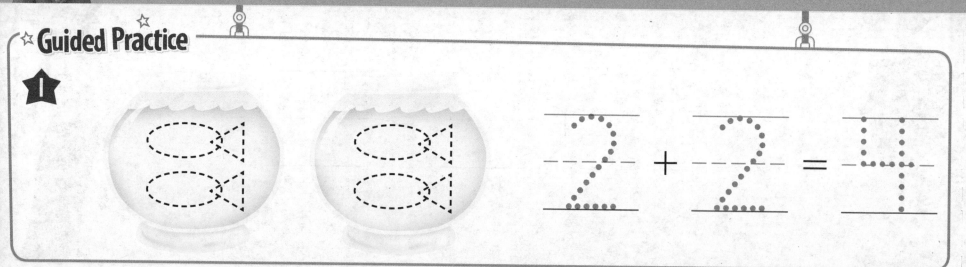

Directions ⬆ Have students listen to the story, and then draw a picture to model what is happening. Then have them write an equation and explain their answer. *Daniel sees 2 fish in one bowl and 2 fish in another bowl. How many fish does he see in all?*

342 three hundred forty-two

Topic 6 | Lesson 10

Independent Practice

2

_____   _____   _____

- - - - -   **+**   - - - - -   **=**   - - - - -

_____   _____   _____

3

_____   _____   _____

- - - - -   **+**   - - - - -   **=**   - - - - -

_____   _____   _____

4

_____   _____   _____

- - - - -   **+**   - - - - -   **=**   - - - - -

_____   _____   _____

5

_____   _____   _____

- - - - -   **+**   - - - - -   **=**   - - - - -

_____   _____   _____

Directions Have students listen to each story, and then draw a picture to model what is happening. Then have them write an equation and explain their answer.  *Julie sees 5 stones in one pail and 3 stones in another pail. How many stones does she see in all?* **3** *A hen laid 2 eggs one day and 3 eggs the next day. How many eggs did she lay in all?* **4** *Maria threw a baseball 5 times in one inning and 2 times in the next inning. How many times did she throw the baseball in all?* **5** *Zak scored 2 goals during a soccer game, and then he scored 4 more goals during another soccer game. How many goals did he score in all?*

Problem Solving

6 7 8

2 + _____ = _____

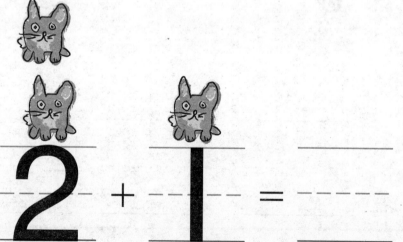

2 + 1 = _____   _____ + _____ = _____

Directions   Read the problem aloud. Then have students use multiple problem-solving methods to solve the problem. Say: *There are 2 rabbits in a hole. The same number of rabbits come in to join them. How many rabbits are there in all?* ⬡ **Reasoning** *What can you answer? How many rabbits join the group?* ⬢ **Explain** *Emily says that the answer is 3 rabbits. Is she right or wrong? Explain how you know.* ⬛ **Model** *Use cubes, draw pictures, or use numbers to show how many rabbits in all. Then write the equation.*

Name _____

Help Tools Games

Another Look!

$$2 + 3 = 5$$

HOME ACTIVITY Help your child make simple drawings to solve addition problems. For example, say: *I had 3 marbles, and then I got 2 more. How many do I have in all? How do you know?*

_____

---- + ---- = ----

_____

---- + ---- = ----

Directions Say: *Carlos finds 2 apples on a tree. Then he finds 3 more on the ground. How many apples does Carlos find in all? Draw the apples, count the apples to find out how many in all, and then write an equation.* Have students listen to each story, and then draw a picture to model what is happening. Then have them write an equation and explain their answer. ★ *There are 4 balls in the box. Paolo puts 1 more ball in the box. How many balls are there in all?* ❷ *Layla has 3 oranges on a plate. Bryce has 3 oranges on a plate. How many oranges do Layla and Bryce have in all?*

_____ _____ _____

_____ = _____ + _____

_____ _____ _____

_____ _____ _____

_____ = _____ + _____

_____ _____ _____

Directions Read the problem aloud. Then have students use multiple problem-solving methods to solve the problem. *Daniel and Carlos each receive 3 flowers. They each put the flowers into vases. Daniel arranges his flowers in a different way than Carlos. Show how the students could have arranged the flowers.* ❸ **Reasoning** *What do you know? How many flowers does each student have?* ❹ **Model** *Use cubes, draw a picture, or use numbers to show two different ways that the students could have arranged their flowers. Then write the equation for each model.* ✋ **Explain** *How do you know that your models are correct? Explain your answer.*

2 ◯ 7

4 + 3 ◯ _____
- - - - - - -
_____

Directions **Understand Vocabulary** Have students: ✪ write the **plus sign** to show addition; ❷ write the **equal sign,** and then complete the equation; ❸ listen to the story, draw a picture to show what is happening, and then write an **equation** to match the story. *Max has 5 yellow cups and 5 orange cups. How many cups does he have in all?*

4

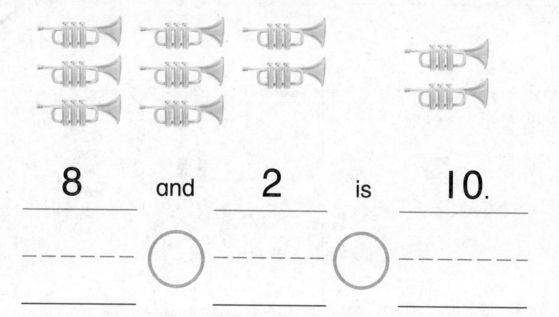

8   and   2   is   10.

—————— ◯ - - - - - ◯ - - - - -
——————   ——————   ——————

- - - - - - -   - - - - - - -   - - - - - - -
        ◯   ◯
——————   ——————   ——————

Topic 6 | Vocabulary Review

Name _____

Set A

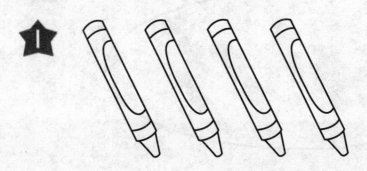

2 and 1 is 3 in all.

⭐ 0 and 4 is _____ in all.

Set B

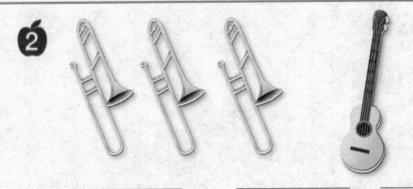

2 and 3 is 5.

_____ and _____ is _____.

Directions Have students: ⭐ listen to the story, color the number of each part, and then write the number to tell how many in all. *Margo has 0 red crayons. She has 4 blue crayons. How many crayons does she have in all?* ❷ add to the first group of instruments, and then write an addition sentence to tell how many in all.

Set C

2 and 3 is 5.

_____   _ _ _ _ _ _ _   _ _ _ _ _ _ _

_____ and _____ is _____ .

Set D

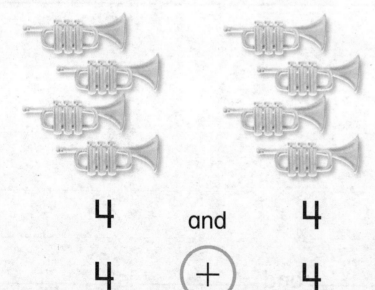

4   and   4

4   (+)   4

2   and   4

_ _ _ _ _   ( )   _ _ _ _ _

Name _____

_____

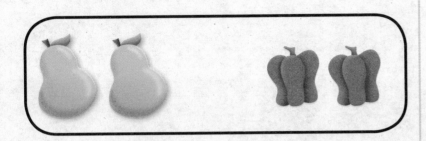

$$2 + 2 = 4$$

_____   _____

- - - - - ◯ - - - - - ◯ - - - - -

_____   _____

_____

🍵 6

$$4 + 3 = 7$$

_____   _____

- - - - - + - - - - = - - - -

_____   _____

Directions Have students: 🖐 use counters to show how to put together the groups, draw a circle around the groups to put them together, and then write an equation to find the sum; 6 listen to the story, use counters to show the addition, draw a picture, and then write an equation to tell how many in all. *Mark has 3 flowers. He picks 2 more flowers. How many flowers does he have in all?*

$6 + 3 = 9$

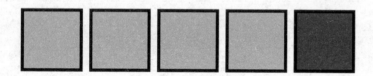

$4 + 1 = 5$

Directions Have students: 🌲 listen to each story, draw a picture to show what is happening, and then write an equation. *Karina puts 4 red balls and 4 purple balls into the toy bin. How many balls are there in all?* 🚩 color a way to make 6, and then write an equation to match the boxes.

Name _____

 1

Ⓐ 1 in all   Ⓒ 4 in all

Ⓑ 6 in all   Ⓓ 8 in all

 2

Ⓐ 1 and 4 is 5.   Ⓒ 1 and 6 is 7.
   1 + 4 = 5   1 + 6 = 7

Ⓑ 1 and 5 is 6.   Ⓓ 1 and 3 is 4.
   1 + 5 = 6   1 + 3 = 4

 3

Ⓐ 2 and 2 is 4.   Ⓒ 2 and 4 is 6.

Ⓑ 2 and 6 is 8.   Ⓓ 2 and 5 is 7.

 4

Ⓐ 3 and 4   Ⓒ 3 and 1
   3 + 4   3 + 1

Ⓑ 4 and 0   Ⓓ 4 and 1
   4 + 0   4 + 1

Directions Have students mark the best answer. **1** *Jen puts 2 teddy bears on her bed. Then she puts 2 more teddy bears on her bed. Which tells how many teddy bears she puts on her bed in all?* **2** *Hayden sees 1 scarecrow, and then he sees 3 more. Which number sentence tells how many scarecrows Hayden sees in all?* **3** *Which sentence tells about adding the groups of tambourines?* **4** *Which tells about the picture?*

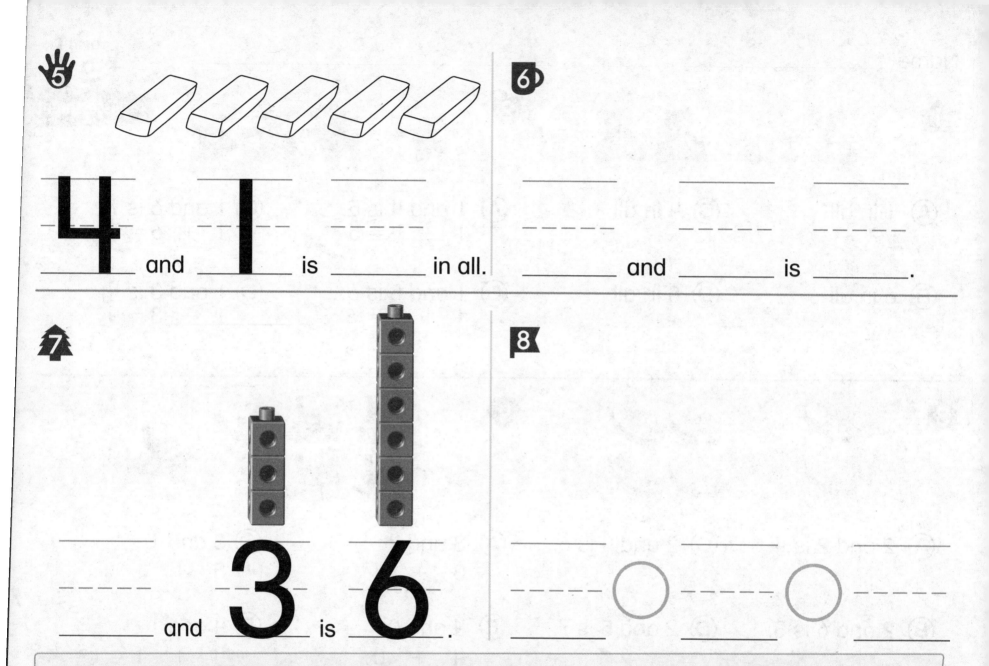

5

4 ____ and 1 ____ is ____ in all.

6

____ and ____ is ____.

7

____ and 3 is 6 ____.

8

____ ◯ ____ ◯ ____

Directions ✋ Have students listen to the story, and then do all of the following to show each part to find how many in all: clap and knock, hold up fingers, and give an explanation of a mental image. Ask them to color the number of each part, and then write the number to tell how many in all. *Ming buys 4 yellow erasers. She buys 1 purple eraser. How many erasers does she buy in all?* **6** Have students draw two groups of carrots to show 8 in all, and then write a number sentence to match the drawing. **7** Have students draw the number of cubes needed to make 6 cubes in all, and then complete the number sentence. **8** Have students listen to the story, use counters to model putting together the groups, draw the counters to show what is happening, and then write an equation for the story. *There are 6 brown bunnies in a garden and 3 white bunnies in the garden. How many bunnies are there in all?*

Topic 6 | Assessment

Name _____

8

🏠 10

5 + 2 = 7

4 + 4 = 8

1 + 7 = 8

Directions Have students: 9 look at the number card, and then draw a circle to put together the groups that show how many in all; 10 match the pictures with the equation that shows the correct parts and how many in all.

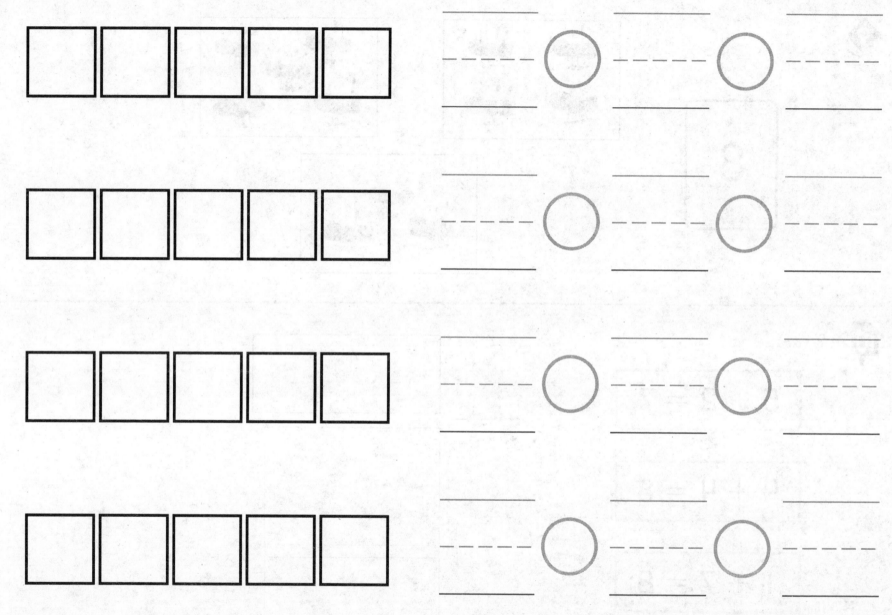

Directions ❈ Have students color the boxes to complete the pattern of ways to make 5, and then write an equation to match the boxes.

356 three hundred fifty-six

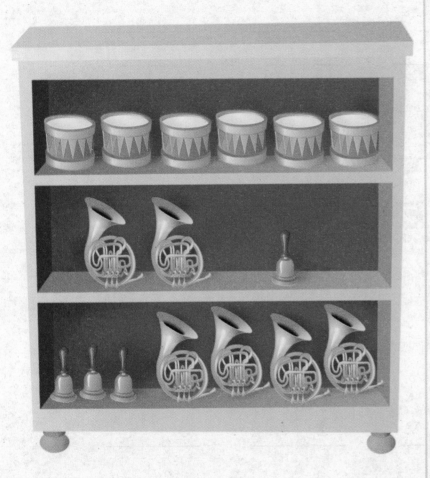

____ ____ ____

____ ____ ____

_____ and _____ is _____ .

2

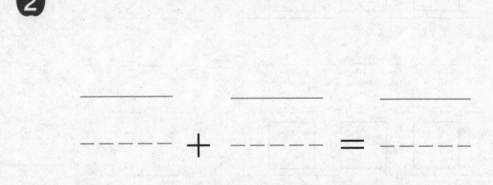

____ ____ ____

____ + ____ = ____

____ ____ ____

Directions **Music Time** Say: *Students play many different instruments in music class.* ★ Say: *How many horns are there?* Have students count on to find the number of horns, and then write an addition sentence to tell how many in all. ❷ Have students add one group of horns to the other group of horns, and then write an equation to find the sum.

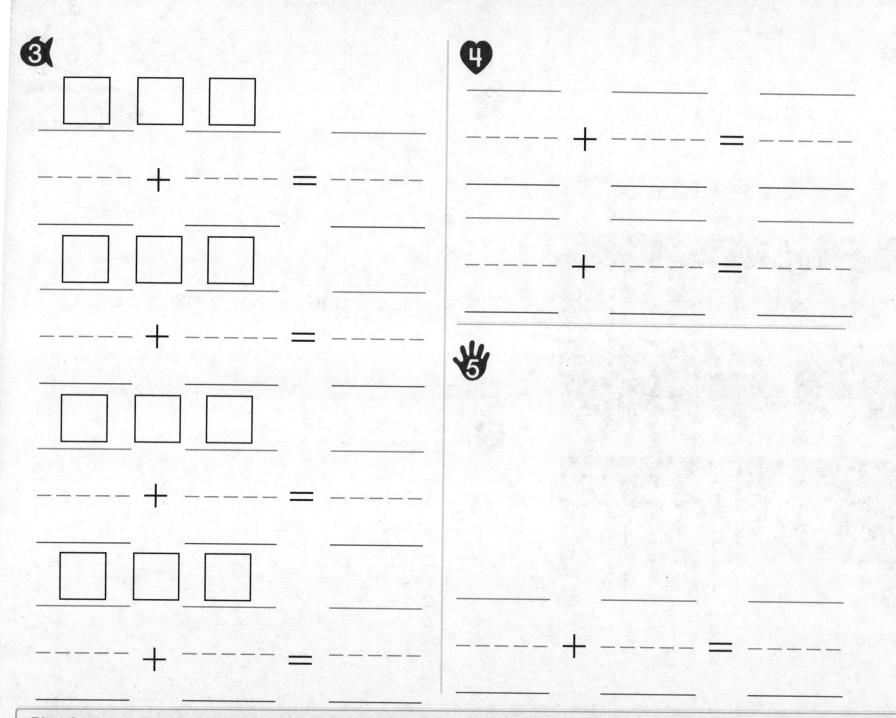

3 ▢ ▢ ▢

⎯⎯ + ⎯⎯ = ⎯⎯

▢ ▢ ▢

⎯⎯ + ⎯⎯ = ⎯⎯

▢ ▢ ▢

⎯⎯ + ⎯⎯ = ⎯⎯

▢ ▢ ▢

⎯⎯ + ⎯⎯ = ⎯⎯

4

⎯⎯ + ⎯⎯ = ⎯⎯

⎯⎯ + ⎯⎯ = ⎯⎯

5

⎯⎯ + ⎯⎯ = ⎯⎯

Directions ❸ Say: *The music teacher puts 3 flutes on the shelves.* Have students color the boxes to complete a pattern to show the different ways she could put the flutes on the shelves. ❹ Say: *The bells on the shelves show one way to make 4.* Have students write an equation to show the way, and then write the matching equation to make 4. ❺ Say: *6 drums are on the shelf. Then Luisa puts more drums on the shelf. Now there are 8 drums on the shelf. How many drums did Luisa put on the shelf?* Have students draw counters to show what is happening, and then complete the equation.

Topic 6 | Performance Assessment

TOPIC 7 Understand Subtraction

Essential Question: How can representing taking apart and taking from in different ways help you learn about subtraction?

Digital Resources

Solve Learn Glossary

Tools Assessment Help Games

Math and Science Project: Animal Needs

Directions Read the character speech bubbles to students. **Find Out!** Have students find out about how plants, animals, and humans use their environment to meet basic needs such as food, water, nutrients, sunlight, space, and shelter. Say: *Different organisms need different things. Talk to friends and relatives about the different needs of plants, animals, and humans, and how different organisms meet those needs.* **Journal: Make a Poster** Have students make a poster. Ask them to draw as many as 5 pictures of a human's needs and as many as 5 pictures of an animal's needs. Have them cross out the needs that are the same for humans and animals, and then write how many are left.

Name _____

❶ $3 + 6 = 9$

❷ $4 + 1 = 5$

❸ $2 + 5 = 7$

_____ _____ _____

- - - - - $+$ - - - - - $=$ - - - - -

_____ _____ _____

_____ _____ _____

- - - - - $+$ - - - - - $=$ - - - - -

_____ _____ _____

❻

_____ _____ _____

- - - - - $+$ - - - - - $=$ - - - - -

_____ _____ _____

Directions Have students: ❶ draw a circle around the plus sign; ❷ draw a circle around the equal sign; ❸ draw a circle around the sum; ❹–❻ count the objects in each group, and then write the equation to tell how many in all.

My Word Cards

Directions Have students cut out the vocabulary cards. Read the front of the card, and then ask them to explain what the word or phrase means.

A-Z
Glossary

left

separate

minus sign (–)

subtract

take away

difference

My Word Cards

Directions Review the definitions and have students study the cards. Extend learning by having students draw pictures for each word on a separate piece of paper.

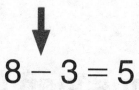

$$8 - 3 = 5$$

Point to the minus sign.
Say: *This is the **minus sign**. It means subtract.*

Point to the cube train.
Say: *When you **separate** groups, you pull or move them apart.*

Point to the jar of marbles.
Say: *There were 6 marbles in the jar. I marble was taken out. There are 5 marbles **left**.*

$$8 - 3 = 5$$

Point to the 5.
Say: *When you subtract, the answer is called the **difference**.*

Point to the 3 swans.
Say: *When you **take away**, you find out how many are left.*

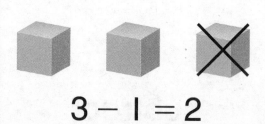

$$3 - 1 = 2$$

Point to the third box.
Say: ***Subtract** means "take away."
3 take away I is 2.*

My Word Cards

Directions Have students cut out the vocabulary cards. Read the front of the card, and then ask them to explain what the word or phrase means.

A-Z
Glossary

subtraction sentence

Directions Review the definitions and have students study the cards. Extend learning by having students draw pictures for each word on a separate piece of paper.

4 take away
3 is 1.

Point to the subtraction sentence. Say: *4 take away 3 is 1 is a* **subtraction sentence**. *It tells how many are left.*

Solve & Share

Directions Say: Marta sees 5 goldfish in the pond. 1 swims away. How many fish are left? Think about the problem in your head. Then act out the story with your fingers to explain. Draw a circle around your answer.

I can ... show numbers in many ways.

I can also model with math.

6 in all   6 in all   6 in all   6 in all

5 are left.

5 are left.

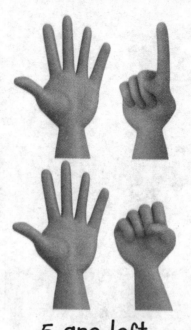

5 are left.

5 are left.

☆ Guided Practice

1   **8** in all   _____ are left.

2   **5** in all   _____ are left.

Directions Have students listen to the story, and then do all of the following to find how many are left: give an explanation of a mental image, use objects to act it out, and hold up fingers. Have them mark Xs on how many birds fly away, and then write the number to tell how many are left.
⭐ *8 eagles sit on a branch. 2 fly away. How many eagles are left?* 🍎 *5 blue jays hop on the ground. I flies away. How many blue jays are left?*

Copyright © Savvas Learning Company LLC. All Rights Reserved.

Topic 7 | Lesson 1

Name _____

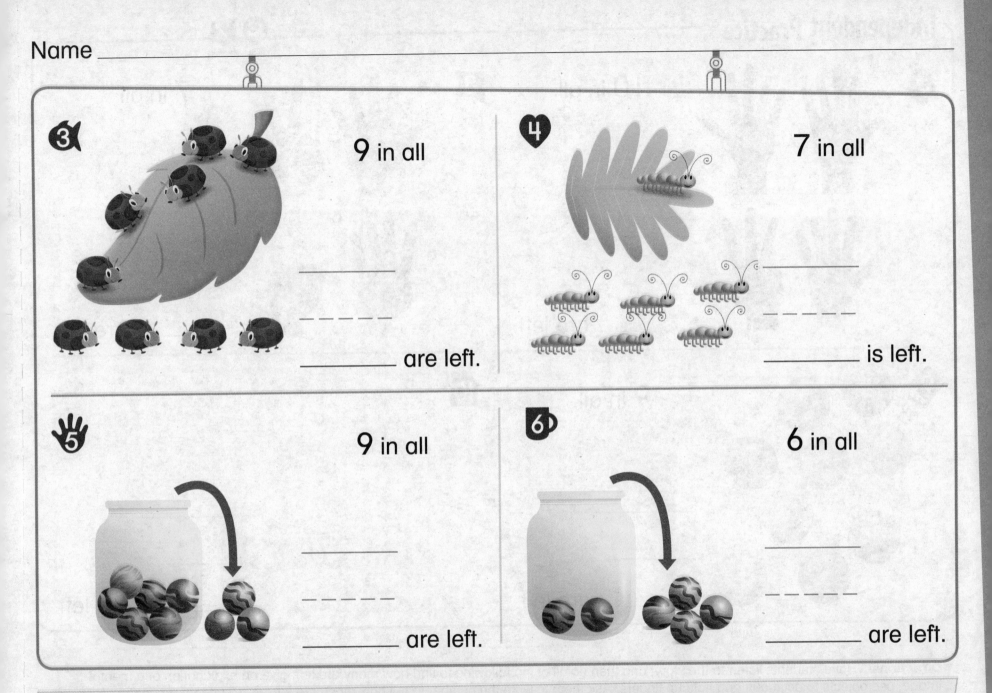

3 9 in all

_____

— — — — —

_____ are left.

4 7 in all

_____

— — — — —

_____ is left.

5 9 in all

_____

— — — — —

_____ are left.

6 6 in all

_____

— — — — —

_____ are left.

Directions Have students listen to the story, and then do all of the following to find how many are left: give an explanation of a mental image, use objects to act it out, and hold up fingers. Have them mark Xs on how many walk away or are taken out, and then write the number to tell how many are left. **3** *9 ladybugs are on a leaf. 4 walk away. How many ladybugs are left?* **4** *7 caterpillars are on a leaf. 6 walk away. How many caterpillars are left?* **5** *9 marbles are in a jar. 3 are taken out. How many marbles are left?* **6** *6 marbles are in a jar. 4 are taken out. How many marbles are left?*

Tools   Assessment

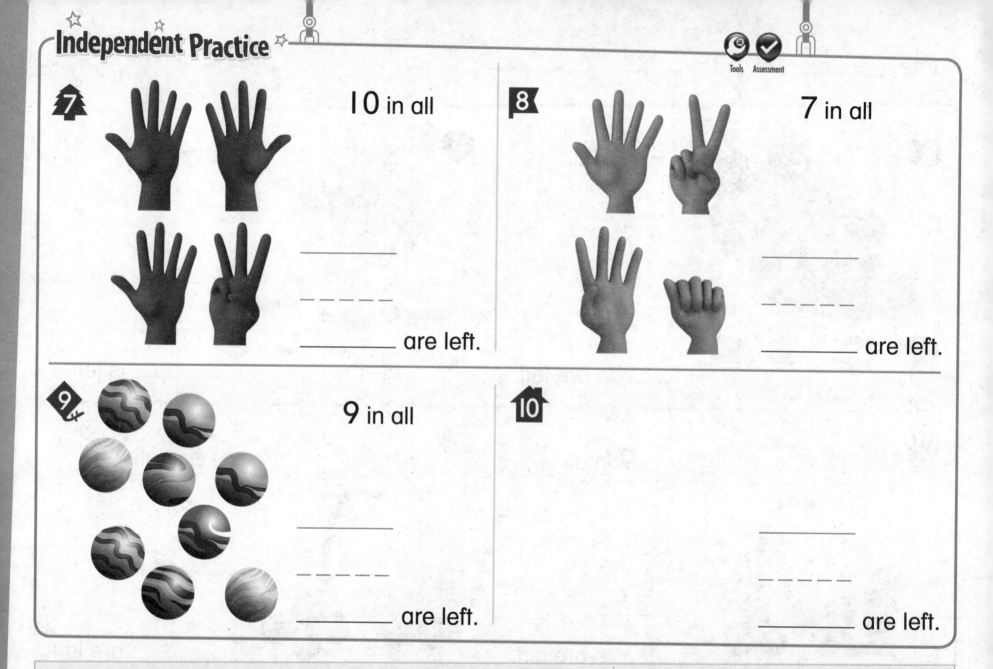

7   10 in all

_____

_ _ _ _ _ _ _ _

_____ are left.

8   7 in all

_____

_ _ _ _ _ _ _ _

_____ are left.

9   9 in all

_____

_ _ _ _ _ _ _ _

_____ are left.

10

_____

_ _ _ _ _ _ _ _

_____ are left.

Directions   Have students listen to the story, and then do all of the following to find how many are left: give an explanation of a mental image, use objects to act it out, and hold up fingers. Ask them to write the number to tell how many are left. 🌲 *10 fingers are in the air. 2 are put down. How many fingers are left?* 🚩 *7 fingers are in the air. 3 are put down. How many fingers are left?* 🔶 Have students listen to the story, and then do all of the following to find how many are left: give an explanation of a mental image, use objects to act it out, and then mark Xs on how many are taken away. Ask them to write the number to tell how many are left. *There are 9 marbles. 6 are taken away. How many marbles are left?* 🏠 **Higher Order Thinking** Have students draw 10 marbles. Have them mark Xs on some of them, and then write the number to tell how many marbles are left.

Name _____

Homework & Practice 7-1
Explore Subtraction

Another Look!

4 are left.

_____ are left.

HOME ACTIVITY Put up to 10 coins on a napkin and have your child count them. Then move some of the coins off of the napkin. Ask: *How many coins are left on the napkin?* Repeat the activity using a different number of coins.

❶

_____
_ _ _ _ _ _
_____ are left.

❷

_____
_ _ _ _ _ _
_____ is left.

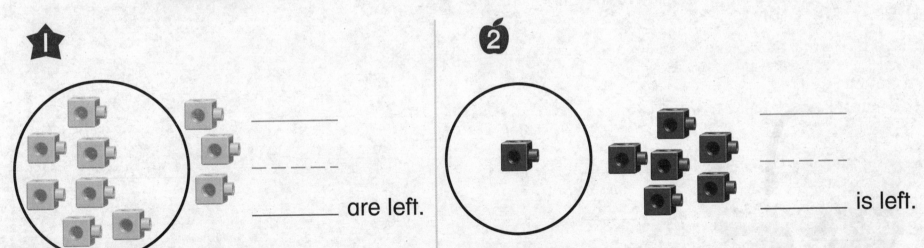

Directions Say: *Carlos puts 8 cubes inside a circle. He moves 4 of them outside the circle.* Model how to explain a mental image, how to act it out with objects, and how to hold up fingers to show how many cubes are left inside the circle. Have students listen to the story, and then do all of the following to find how many are left: give an explanation of a mental image, use objects to act it out, and hold up fingers. Have them write the number to tell how many are left. ❶ *Carlos puts 10 cubes inside a circle. He moves 3 of them out. How many cubes are left?* ❷ *Carlos puts 7 cubes inside a circle. He moves 6 of them out. How many cubes are left?*

3 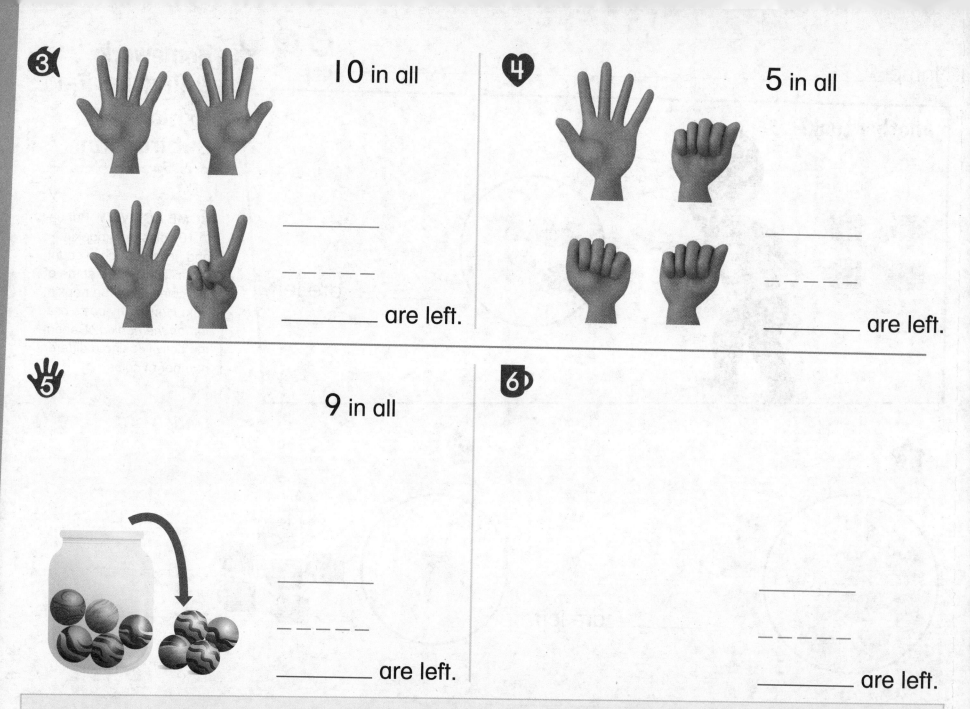 10 in all

_____

_____ are left.

4 5 in all

_____

_____ are left.

5 9 in all

_____

_____ are left.

6

_____

_____ are left.

Directions Have students listen to the story, and then do all of the following to find how many are left: give an explanation of a mental image, use objects to act it out, and hold up fingers. Ask them to write the number to tell how many are left. **3** _10 fingers are in the air. 3 are put down. How many fingers are left?_ **4** _5 fingers are in the air. 5 are put down. How many fingers are left?_ **5** _9 marbles are in a jar. 4 are taken out. How many marbles are left?_ **6** **Higher Order Thinking** Have students draw 8 marbles. Have them mark Xs on some of them, and then write the number to tell how many marbles are left.

Topic 7 | Lesson 1

Solve & Share

Name _____

_____   _____

Directions Say: *Alex picks 7 apples. Some apples are red, and some are yellow. Alex wants to put the red apples in one basket and the yellow in the other. How many red apples and how many yellow apples can there be? Write the numbers to tell how many. Draw pictures to show your answer.*

I can ...
take apart a number and tell the parts.

I can also reason about math.

Learn Glossary

Take apart 7.

Take apart 7.

Take apart 7.

2   and   5

☆ Guided Practice

1   Take apart 5.

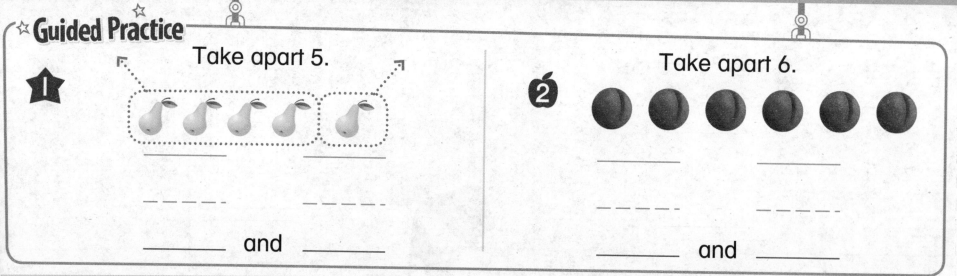

_____   _____

_ _ _ _ _   _ _ _ _ _

_____ and _____

2   Take apart 6.

_____   _____

_ _ _ _ _   _ _ _ _ _

_____ and _____

Directions Have students: **1** take apart the group of pears. Then have them draw a circle around the parts they made, and then write the numbers to tell the parts; **2** take apart the group of peaches. Then have them draw a circle around the parts they made, and then write the numbers to tell the parts.

372 three hundred seventy-two

Name _____

⭐ 3   Take apart 4.

_____ _____

- - - - - - -   - - - - - - -

_____ and _____

💙 4   Take apart 10.

_____ _____

- - - - - - -   - - - - - - -

_____ and _____

✋ 5   Take apart 3.

_____ _____

- - - - - - -   - - - - - - -

_____ and _____

☕ 6   Take apart 8.

_____ _____

- - - - - - -   - - - - - - -

_____ and _____

Directions ⭐–☕ Have students take apart the group of fruit. Then have them draw a circle around the parts they made, and then write the numbers to tell the parts.

Independent Practice

7 Take apart 6.

_____   _____

- - - - -   - - - -

_____   and   _____

8 Take apart 2.

_____   _____

- - - - -   - - - - -

_____   and   _____

9 Take apart 5.

_____   _____

- - - - -   - - - - -

_____   and   _____

10 _____

- - - - -

Take apart _____ .

_____   _____

- - - - -   - - - - -

_____   and   _____

Directions 🌲 and 🚩 Have students take apart the group of fruit. Then have them draw a circle around the parts they made, and then write the numbers to tell the parts. ♦ **Higher Order Thinking** Have students draw counters to show a group of 5. Then have them take apart the group of counters, draw a circle around the parts they made, and then write the numbers to tell the parts. 🏠 **Higher Order Thinking** Have students choose any number between 2 and 10, write that number on the top line, and then draw a group of counters to show that number. Have them take apart the group of counters, draw a circle around the parts they made, and then write the numbers to tell the parts.

Name _____

Another Look!

Take apart 9.

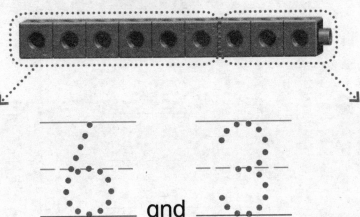

6 and 3

HOME ACTIVITY Give your child 8 coins. Have him or her use the coins to show a way to take apart 8 into two parts. Then have them write the parts.

⭐ Take apart 6.

_____ _____

_____ and _____

🍎 Take apart 7.

_____ _____

_____ and _____

Directions Say: *Carlos takes apart his cube train. He makes a group of 6 and a group of 3. Draw circles around the cubes to show the parts he made, and then write the numbers to tell the parts.* ⭐ and 🍎 Have students take apart each cube train. Have them draw a circle around the parts they made, and then write the numbers to tell the parts.

③

Take apart 8.

_____   _____

_ _ _ _ _   _ _ _ _ _

_____ and _____

Take apart 8.

_____   _____

_ _ _ _ _   _ _ _ _ _

_____ and _____

④

_____   _____

_ _ _ _ _   _ _ _ _ _

_____ and _____

_____   _____

_ _ _ _ _   _ _ _ _ _

_____ and _____

Directions ❸ Have students take apart the cube train on the left. Have them draw a circle around the parts they made, and then write the numbers to tell the parts. Have them show a different way to take apart the cube train on the right, draw a circle around the parts they made, and then write the numbers to tell the parts. ❹ **Higher Order Thinking** Have students draw two cube trains with the same amount of cubes. Have them take apart the cube trains in two different ways, draw a circle around the parts they made, and then write the numbers to tell the parts.

376 three hundred seventy-six

Name _____

_____   _____

_____   _____   _____

_____ take away _____ is _____.

Directions Say: *Marta is watching bugs. She sees 4 ladybugs. Then 2 crawl away. How can you complete the sentence to tell how many ladybugs are left?*

I can ...
represent subtraction as
taking away from a whole.

I can also make
sense of problems.

3 take away 1 is 2.

Guided Practice

1 6 take away 3 is 3.

2 ___ take away ___ is ___.

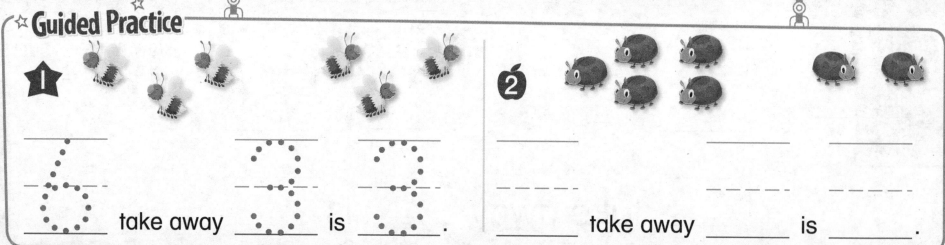

Directions Have students listen to each story, and then complete the sentence to tell how many bugs are left. **1** *Marta sees 6 bumblebees. 3 leave. How many bumblebees are left?* **2** *Marta sees 7 ladybugs. 2 leave. How many ladybugs are left?*

Name _____

3 🐦

_____   take away _____   is _____ .

4 ❤️

_____   take away _____   is _____ .

5 ✋

_____   take away _____   is _____ .

6 ☕

_____   take away _____   is _____ .

Directions Have students listen to each story, and then complete the sentence to tell how many bugs are left. **3** *Emily sees 6 grasshoppers on the table. 2 hop away. How many grasshoppers are left?* **4** *Emily sees 7 dragonflies. 3 fly away. How many dragonflies are left?* **5** *Emily sees 8 caterpillars resting on a branch. 4 crawl away. How many caterpillars are left?* **6** **Math and Science** Say: *Ants can move material much bigger than themselves. Emily sees 10 ants on a picnic blanket. 4 walk away. How many ants are left?*

Topic 7 | Lesson 3

three hundred seventy-nine **379**

Independent Practice

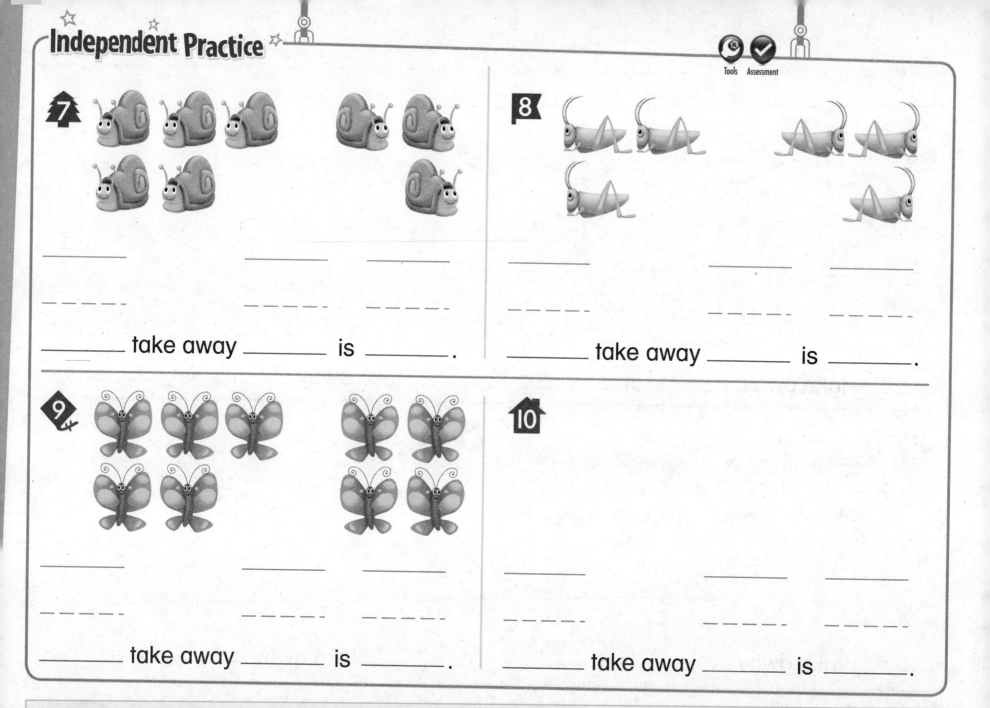

7 _____ take away _____ is _____ .

8 _____ take away _____ is _____ .

9 _____ take away _____ is _____ .

10 _____ take away _____ is _____ .

Directions Have students listen to each story, and then complete the sentence to tell how many are left. **7** *Jerome sees 8 snails on the sidewalk. 3 slink away. How many snails are left?* **8** *Jerome sees 6 grasshoppers in the grass. 3 hop away. How many grasshoppers are left?* **9** *Jerome sees 9 butterflies in the garden. 4 flutter away. How many butterflies are left?* **10** **Higher Order Thinking** *Have students listen to the story, draw a picture to show the story, and then complete the sentence to tell how many are left. Jerome sees 7 inchworms on a tree. 4 crawl away. How many inchworms are left?*

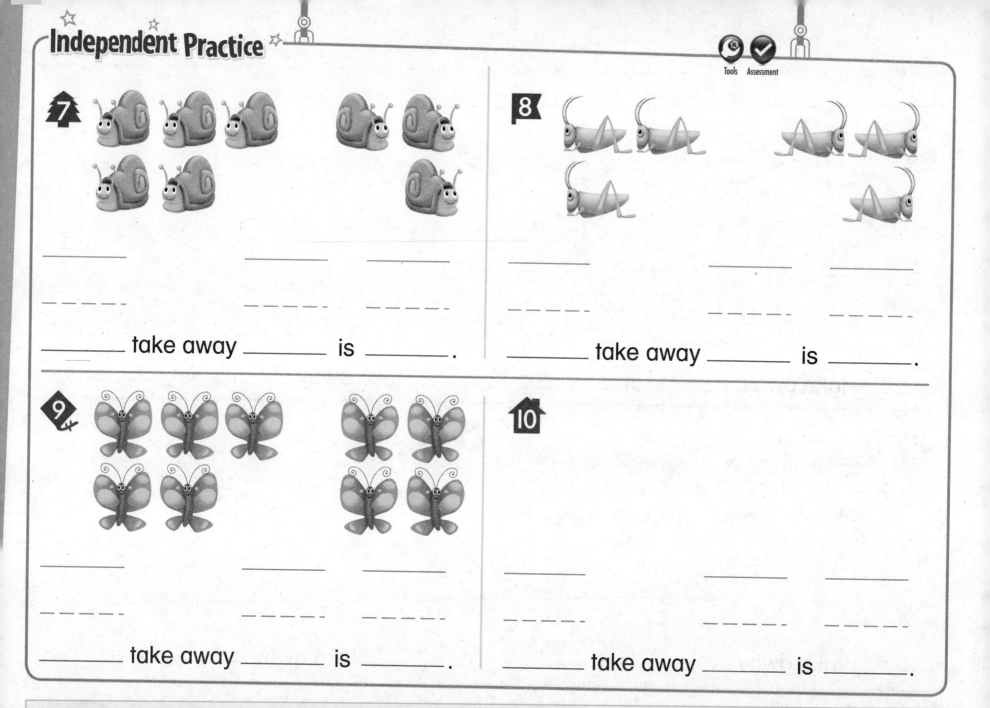

380 three hundred eighty

Topic 7 | Lesson 3

Name _____

Another Look!

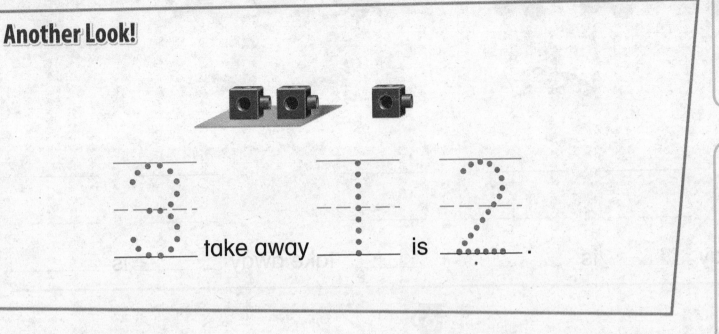

3 take away 1 is 2.

HOME ACTIVITY Place 7 toys or other small objects in front of your child. Ask him or her to tell you how many toys there are in all, and then move 3 of the toys to the side and tell how many toys are left. Have your child say a sentence that tells how many are left.

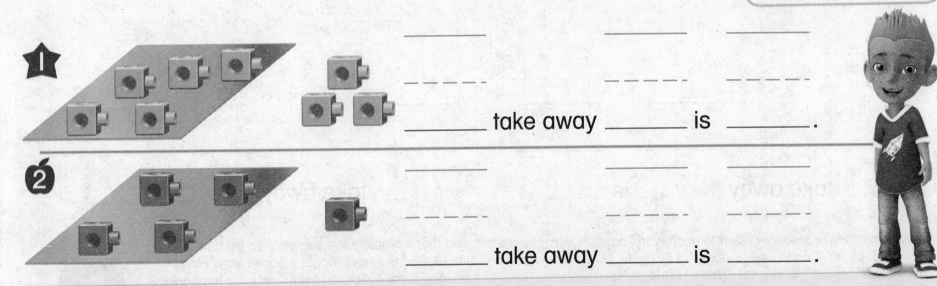

⭐ _____ take away _____ is _____.

② _____ take away _____ is _____.

Directions Say: *There are 3 cubes on a mat. Then Alex moves 1 away. How many cubes are left on the mat? Complete the sentence to tell how many are left. Have students listen to each story, and then complete the sentence to tell how many are left.* ⭐ *Alex puts 8 cubes on a mat. Then he moves 3 away. How many cubes are left on the mat?* ② *Alex puts 5 cubes on a mat. Then he moves 1 away. How many cubes are left on the mat?*

3

_____   _____

‐ ‐ ‐ ‐ ‐   ‐ ‐ ‐ ‐ ‐

_____ take away _____ is _____.

4

_____   _____

‐ ‐ ‐ ‐ ‐   ‐ ‐ ‐ ‐ ‐

_____ take away _____ is _____.

5

_____   _____

‐ ‐ ‐ ‐ ‐   ‐ ‐ ‐ ‐ ‐

_____ take away _____ is _____.

6

_____   _____

‐ ‐ ‐ ‐ ‐   ‐ ‐ ‐ ‐ ‐

_____ take away _____ is _____.

Directions Have students listen to each story, count how many are left, and then complete the sentence to tell how many are left. **3** *Carlos sees 6 ducks. 3 fly away. How many ducks are left?* **4** *Carlos sees 6 frogs. 1 hops away. How many frogs are left?* **5 Higher Order Thinking** Have students listen to the story, draw a picture to show what is happening, and then complete the sentence to tell how many are left. *Carlos sees 6 ants. 4 crawl away. How many ants are left?* **6 Higher Order Thinking** Have students listen to the story, draw a picture to show what is happening, and then complete the sentence to tell how many are left. *Some oranges are on Carlos's plate. He eats 2 oranges. 4 are left. How many oranges were on the plate before Carlos ate some?*

Topic 7 | Lesson 3

Solve & Share

Solve

Directions Say: *There are 5 parrots in a tree. 2 fly away. Use counters or draw pictures to show how many parrots are left. Explain how you know you are correct.*

I can ... separate numbers.

I can also reason about math.

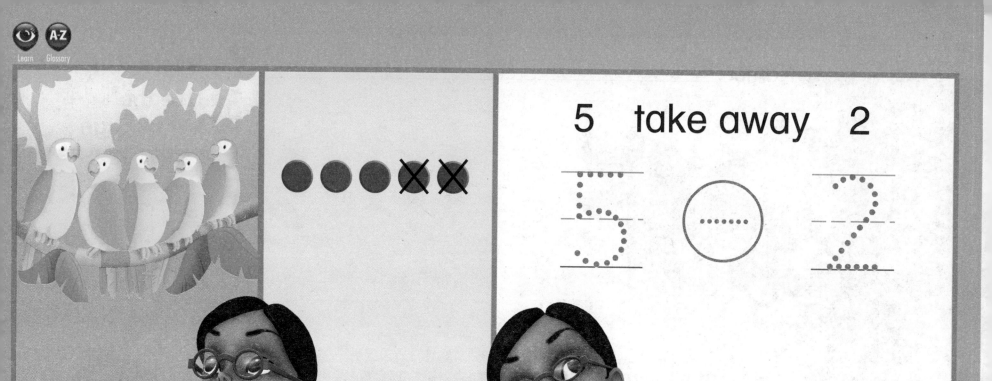

5   take away   2

5 ◯ 2

☆ **Guided Practice**

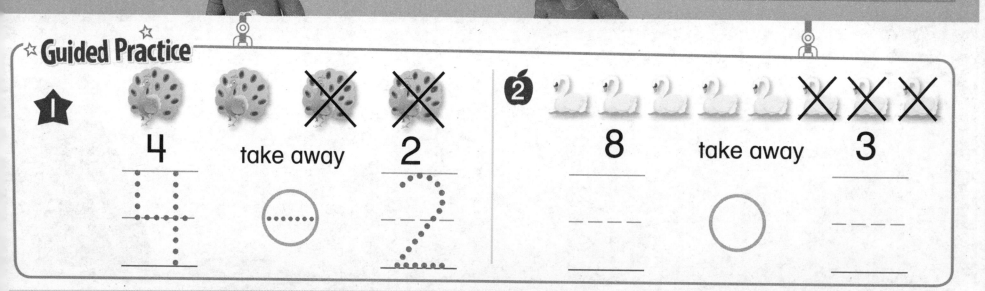

1.

4   take away   2

4 ◯ 2

2.

8   take away   3

8 ◯ 3

Directions 1 and 2 Have students count the birds and write the number to tell how many, and then write the minus sign and the number subtracted.

384 three hundred eighty-four

Topic 7 | Lesson 4

Name _____

3

6   take away   2

_ _ _ _   ◯   _ _ _ _

4

7   take away   3

_ _ _ _   ◯   _ _ _ _

5

8   take away   3

_ _ _ _   ◯   _ _ _ _

6

9   take away   4

_ _ _ _   ◯   _ _ _ _

Directions 3—6 Have students count the birds and write the number to tell how many, and then write the minus sign and the number subtracted.

Topic 7 | Lesson 4

three hundred eighty-five   **385**

Independent Practice

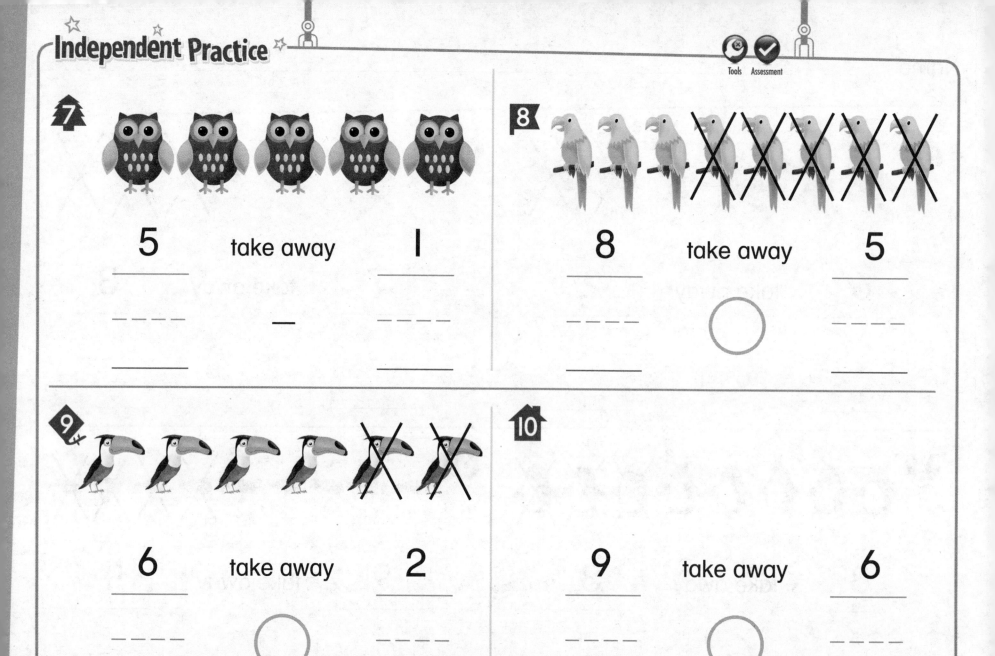

7

5   take away   1

___   —   _ _ _

___

8

8   take away   5

_ _ _   ◯   _ _ _

___

9

6   take away   2

_ _ _   ◯   _ _ _

10

9   take away   6

_ _ _ _   ◯   _ _ _ _

Directions 🌲 **Vocabulary** Have students listen to the story, and then show how a **minus sign** is represented by marking an X on the owl that flies away. Have them write a number to tell how many and the number subtracted. *There are 5 owls. 1 flies away.* 🏴 and 🦤 Have students count the birds and write the number to tell how many, and then write the minus sign and the number subtracted. 🏠 **Higher Order Thinking** Have students listen to the story, draw counters and mark Xs to show the subtraction, and then write the numbers and the minus sign to solve. *There are 9 birds. Some fly away. 3 birds are left.*

       Topic 7 | Lesson 4

Name _____

Another Look!

6   take away   3

HOME ACTIVITY Have your child point to a minus sign on the page and explain what the minus sign means. Then encourage him or her to tell some number stories that involve subtracting.

⭐ 1

7   take away   5

🍎 2

5   take away   4

Directions Say: *Write the number to tell how many counters in all, and then write the minus sign. How many counters are subtracted? Write the number to tell how many are subtracted.* ⭐ and 🍎 Have students count the counters and write the number to tell how many, write the minus sign, and then count the counters that are taken away and write the number.

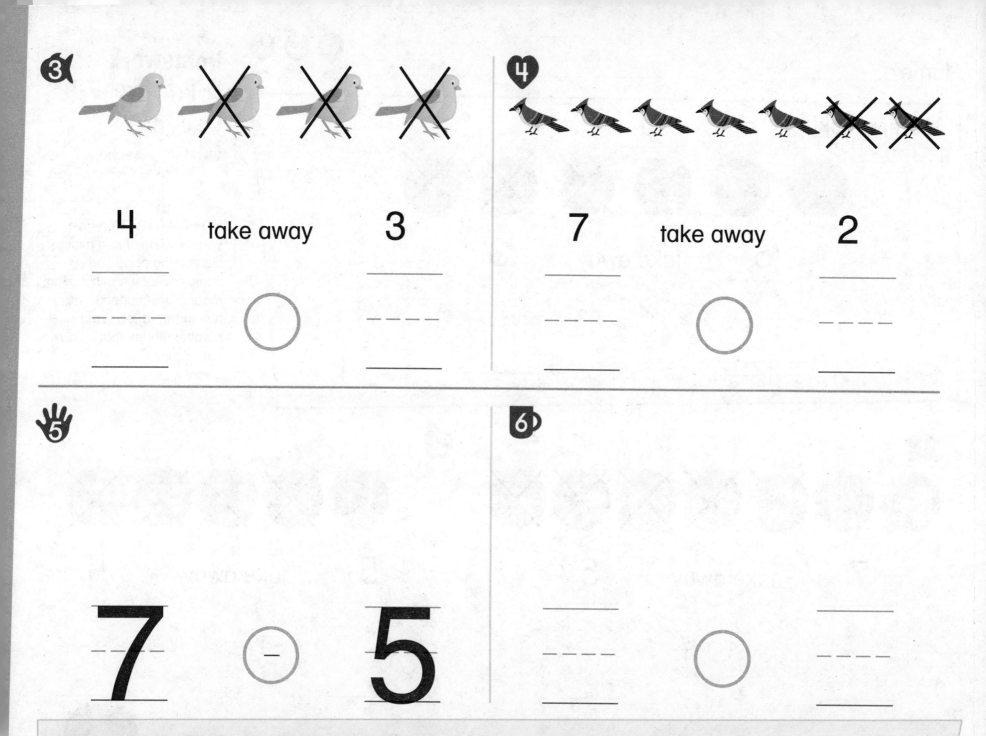

3

4   take away   3

___ ( ) - - -

- - -   ___

4

7   take away   2

___ ( ) - - -

- - -   ___

5

7 (-) **5**

6

- - - ( ) - - -

___   ___

Directions **3** and **4** Have students count the birds and write the number to tell how many, and then write the minus sign and the number subtracted. **5 Higher Order Thinking** Have students draw a picture to match the number sentence. **6 Higher Order Thinking** Have students listen to the story, draw counters and mark Xs to show what is happening, and then write the numbers and the minus sign. *There are 6 parrots in a cage. A zookeeper takes some away for a show. 2 parrots are left in the cage.*

Solve & Share

Name _____

Solve

Directions Say: *There are 6 fire hats. Firefighters take 3 away. What numbers do you subtract to find how many hats are left? How can you show the subtraction?*

I can ...
separate more numbers.

I can also reason about math.

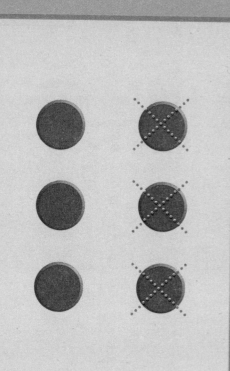

6 take away 3 is 3.

6 − 3 = 3

☆ Guided Practice

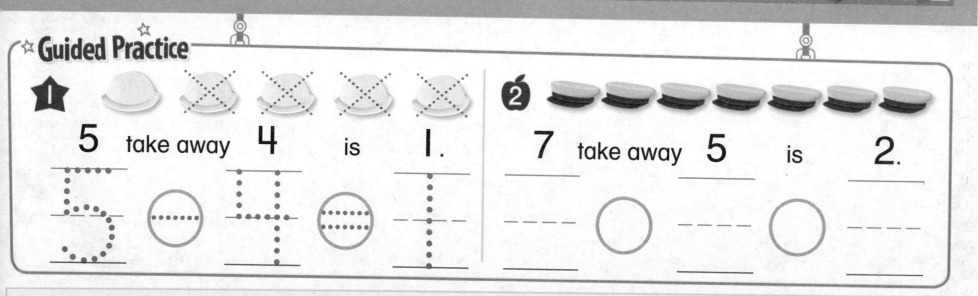

★1

5 take away 4 is 1.

②

7 take away 5 is 2.

Directions ★ and ② Have students use counters to model the problem, mark Xs to subtract, and then write a subtraction equation to find the difference.

Name _____

3 ⟲

8 take away 2 is 6.

_____ ◯ _____ ◯ _____

_____

4 ♥

6 take away 5 is 1.

_____ ◯ _____ ◯ _____

_____

5 ✋

9 take away 5 is 4.

_____ ◯ _____ ◯ _____

_____

6 ☕

7 take away 2 is 5.

_____ ◯ _____ ◯ _____

_____

Directions **3**–**6** Have students use counters to model the problem, mark Xs to subtract, and then write an equation to find the difference.

Independent Practice

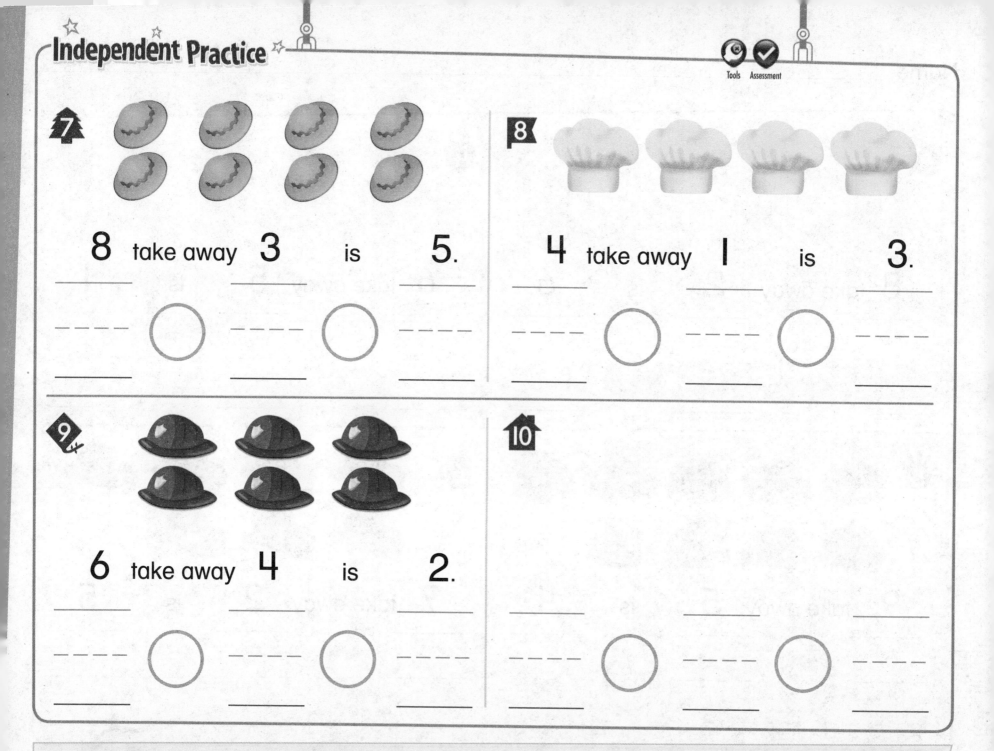

7 8 take away 3 is 5.

_____ ◯ _____ ◯ _____

8 4 take away 1 is 3.

_____ ◯ _____ ◯ _____

9 6 take away 4 is 2.

_____ ◯ _____ ◯ _____

10

_____ ◯ _____ ◯ _____

Directions 7–9 Have students use counters to model the problem, mark Xs to subtract, and then write an equation to find the difference.
10 Higher Order Thinking Have students listen to the story, draw counters and mark Xs to show the problem, and then write an equation to find the difference. *There are 7 baseball caps. Some are worn to a game. There are 4 left. How many caps were worn to the game?*

Name _____

Help Tools Games

Another Look!

7 take away 4 is 3.

7 − 6 = 3

HOME ACTIVITY Have your child point to the difference in a number sentence on this page and explain the number. Then give your child 4 toys and help him or her tell a subtracting story. Ask him or her to find the difference. Repeat with other numbers and objects.

6 take away 4 is 2.

___ ___ ___

 2

4 take away 3 is 1.

___ ___ ___

Directions Say: *What numbers are being subtracted? Mark Xs on the counters to show how many to take away, and then write the numbers, the minus sign, the equal sign, and the difference to write the equation.* ⭐ and ❷ *Have students mark Xs to show how many counters to take away, and then write an equation to find the difference.*

Topic 7 | Lesson 5

Digital Resources at SavvasRealize.com

three hundred ninety-three **393**

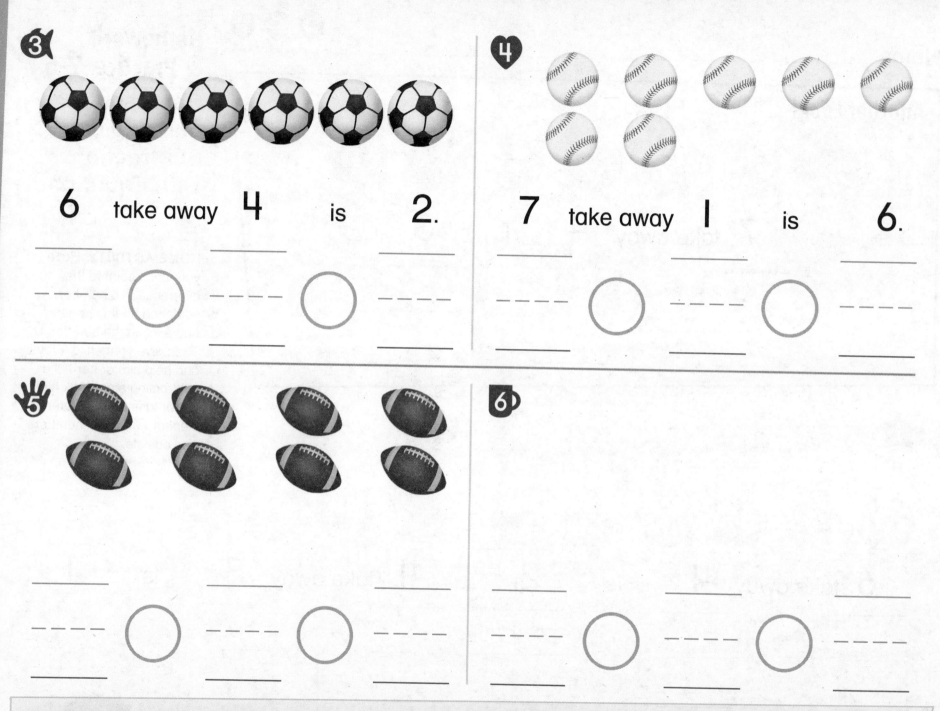

3

6   take away   4   is   2.

___ ___ ⃝ ___ ___ ⃝ ___ ___

4

7   take away   1   is   6.

___ ___ ⃝ ___ ___ ⃝ ___ ___

5

___ ___ ⃝ ___ ___ ⃝ ___ ___

6

___ ___ ⃝ ___ ___ ⃝ ___ ___

Directions **3** and **4** Have students mark Xs to subtract, and then write an equation to find the difference. **5 Higher Order Thinking** Have students write how many balls there are in all, choose a number to subtract, mark Xs to show how many to take away, and then write the equation to find the difference. **6 Higher Order Thinking** Have students listen to the story, draw counters and mark Xs to show the problem, and then write an equation to find the difference. *Some baseballs are in a bag. 3 are taken out. There are 6 baseballs left.*

Topic 7 | Lesson 5

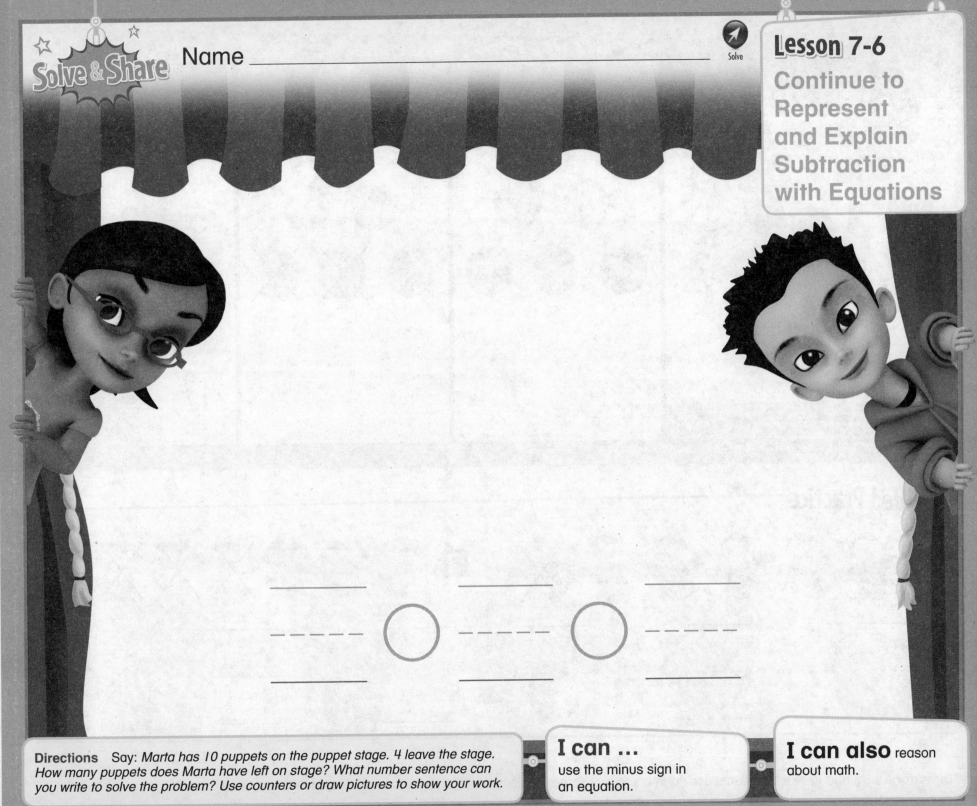

Solve & Share

Name _____

Solve

----- ◯ ----- ◯ -----

Directions Say: *Marta has 10 puppets on the puppet stage. 4 leave the stage. How many puppets does Marta have left on stage? What number sentence can you write to solve the problem? Use counters or draw pictures to show your work.*

I can ...
use the minus sign in an equation.

I can also reason about math.

Digital Resources at SavvasRealize.com

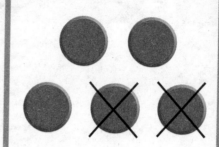

$5 - 2 = 3$

☆ Guided Practice

1

6 − 1 = 5

2

___ ___ ○ ___ ___ ○ ___ ___

___   ___   ___

Directions 🌟 and ❷ Have students use counters to model the problem, and then write an equation to tell how many are left.

Name _____

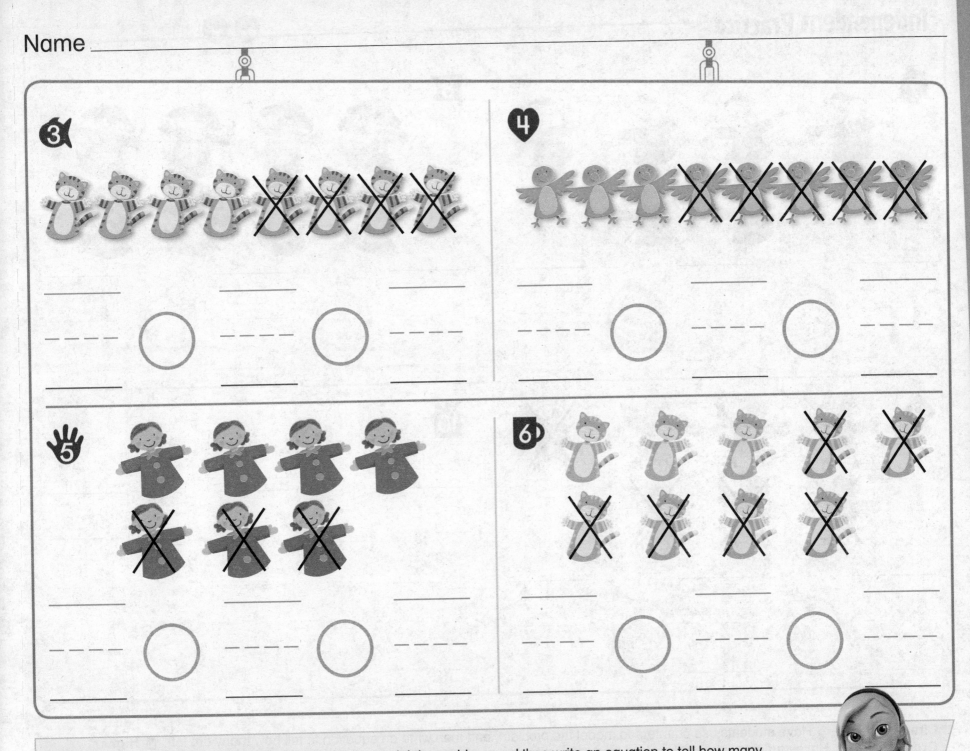

Directions ❸–❻ Have students use counters to model the problem, and then write an equation to tell how many are left.

Independent Practice

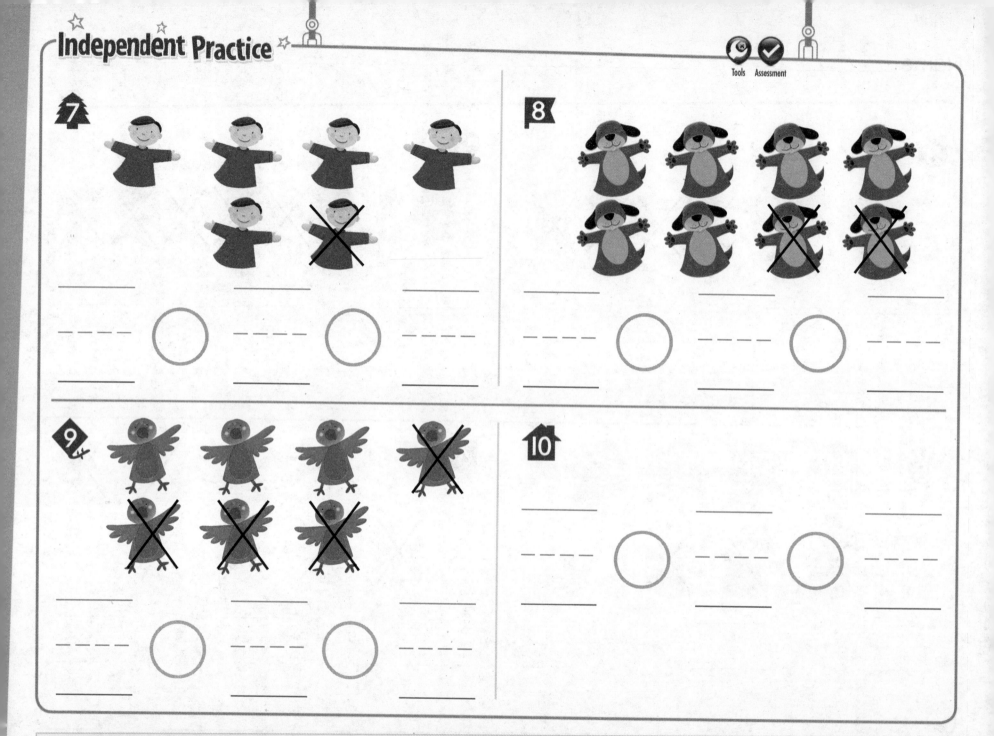

7 ___ ___ ___ ◯ ___ ___ ___ ◯ ___ ___ ___

8 ___ ___ ___ ◯ ___ ___ ___ ◯ ___ ___ ___

9 ___ ___ ___ ◯ ___ ___ ___ ◯ ___ ___ ___

10 ___ ___ ___ ◯ ___ ___ ___ ◯ ___ ___ ___

Directions ★ – ★ Have students use counters to model the problem, and then write an equation to tell how many are left. **10 Higher Order Thinking** Have students listen to the story, and then write an equation to tell how many are left. *Marta has 8 puppets for the puppet show. She takes away some puppets to be fixed. Marta has 5 left for the show. How many puppets did she take away?*

Name _____

Another Look!

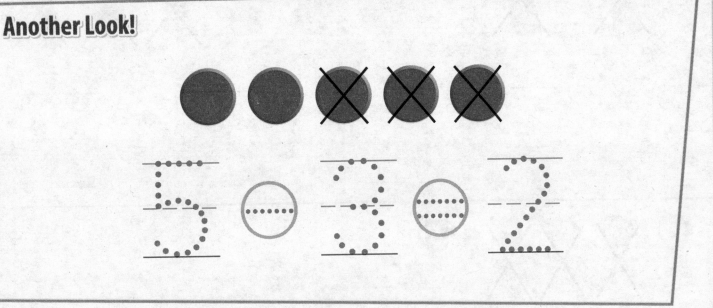

$$5 - 3 = 2$$

HOME ACTIVITY Give your child 6 small objects and ask him or her to give you 3 of the objects. Ask your child to tell what he or she did and to write an equation (6 − 3 = 3). Repeat the activity, using other subtraction situations.

Directions Say: *How many counters are there in all? How many counters are being subtracted? How many are left? Write the numbers, the minus sign, the equal sign, and the difference to complete the equation.* ⭐ and 🍎 Have students subtract the group of counters that are marked with Xs, and then write an equation to tell how many are left.

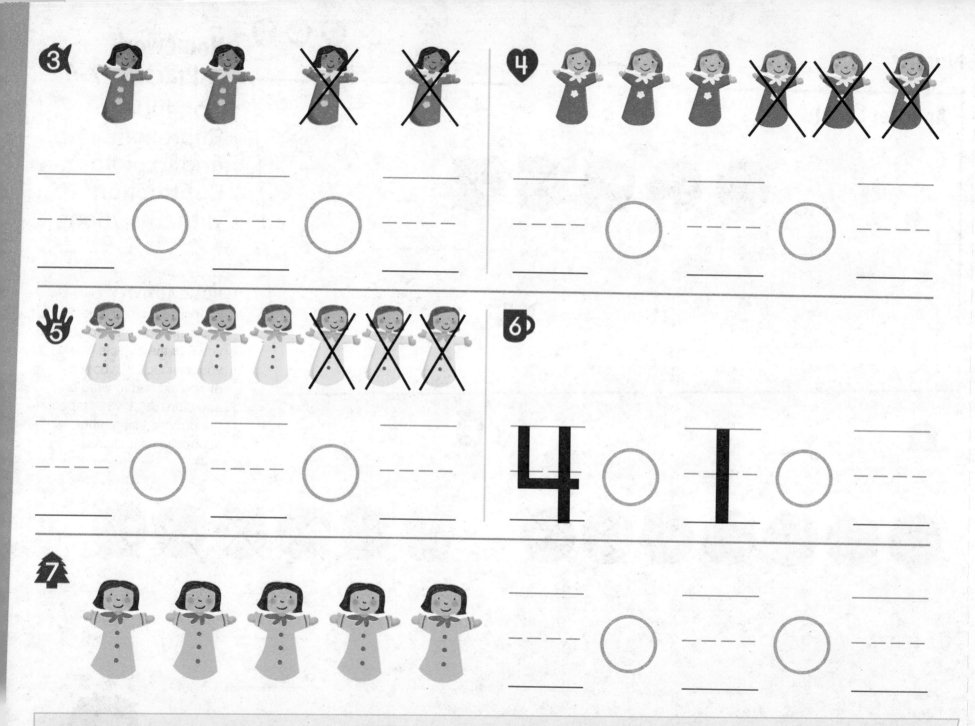

3 ____ ◯ ____ ◯ ____

4 ____ ◯ ____ ◯ ____

5 ____ ◯ ____ ◯ ____

6 4 ◯ 1 ◯ ____

7 ____ ◯ ____ ◯ ____

Directions **3–5** Have students write an equation to tell how many are left. **6 Higher Order Thinking** Have students draw a picture to show the subtraction, and then complete the equation to find the difference. **7 Higher Order Thinking** Have students listen to the story, mark Xs to show what is happening, and then write an equation to tell how many are left. *Marta has some puppets. She gives 2 puppets to her brother. She has 3 left. How many puppets did she have before?*

Solve & Share

Name _____

Solve

Directions Say: *Marta's dog, Spot, loves to eat doggie biscuits. Marta put 6 biscuits in a bag. One day, Spot ate 4 biscuits. Now there are only 2 left. How does Marta know there are 2 biscuits left? Use counters, pictures, or numbers to explain and show your work.*

I can ...
find the difference of two numbers.

I can also make math arguments.

Digital Resources at SavvasRealize.com

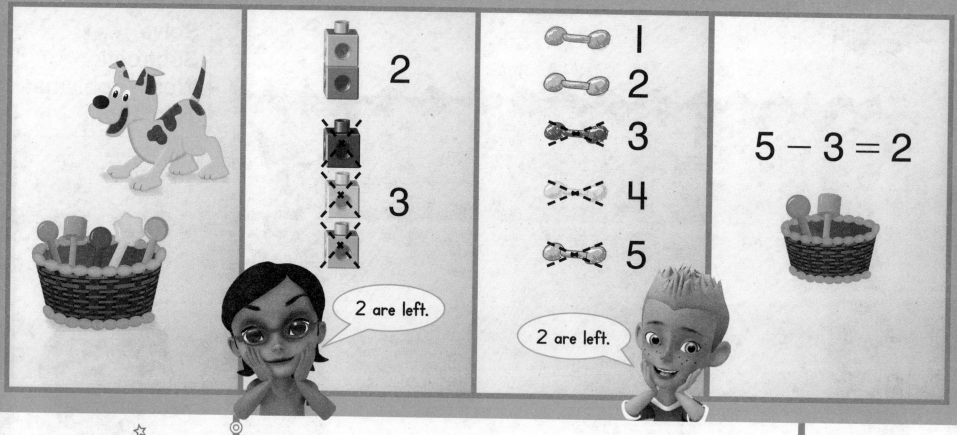

2

3

2 are left.

$$5 - 3 = 2$$

1
2
3
4
5

2 are left.

☆ Guided Practice

 1

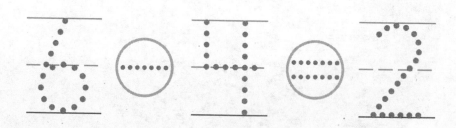

Directions ⬆ Have students listen to the story, draw a picture to show what is happening, and then write a subtraction equation. Then have them explain their work aloud. Say: *Marta has 6 kittens. She gives them a big bowl of water to drink. But there is only room for 4 kittens to drink at the same time. How does Marta know that 2 kittens have to wait?*

Name _____

2

_____ ◯ _____ ◯ _____

3

_____ ◯ _____ ◯ _____

4

_____ ◯ _____ ◯ _____

5

_____ ◯ _____ ◯ _____

Directions Have students listen to each story, draw a picture to show what is happening, and then write an equation. Then have them explain their work aloud. **2** *Emily sees 8 rabbits in a pet store. Someone buys 3 of them. How many rabbits are left?* **3** *Emily sees 7 birds in a cage. The pet store owner opens the cage door and 3 fly out. How many birds are left?* **4** *Emily sees 8 puppies in the store. 6 of them are sold. How many puppies are left?* **5** *Emily sees 5 hamsters sleeping. 1 leaves to eat. How many hamsters are left?*

Independent Practice

Tools Assessment

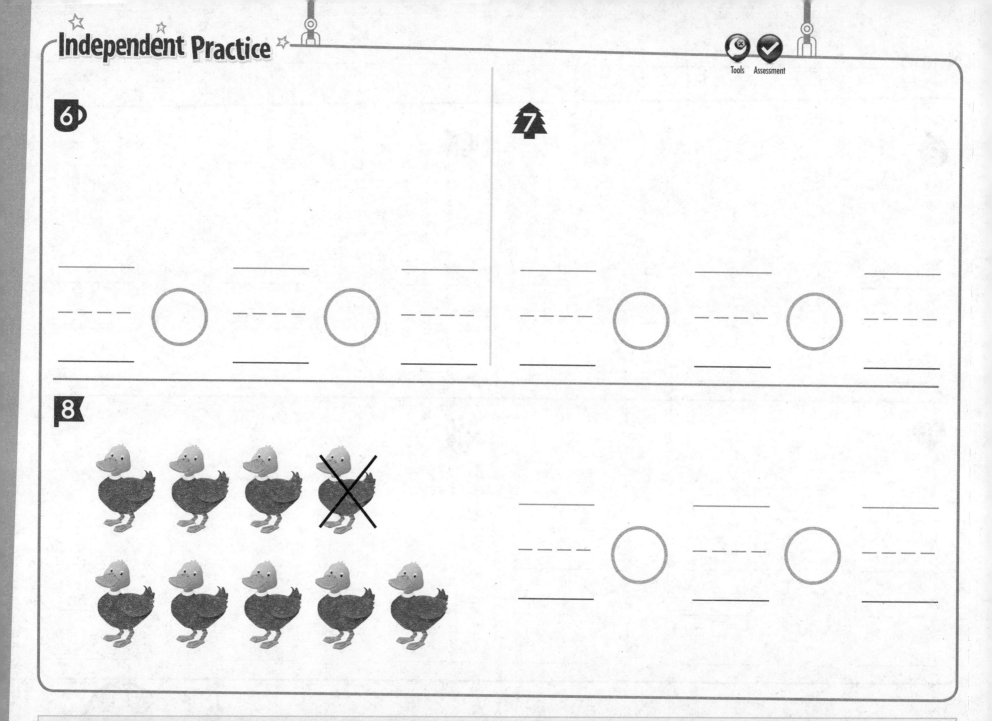

Directions Have students listen to each story, draw a picture to show what is happening, and then write an equation. **6** *There are 6 birds in a birdbath. 4 fly away. How many birds are left?* **7** *There are 5 acorns under a tree. A squirrel takes 3 of them. How many acorns are left?* **8 Higher Order Thinking** Have students listen to the story, draw a circle around the picture that shows the story and tell why the other picture does NOT show the story, and then write an equation. *There are 4 ducks in a pond. 1 leaves. How many ducks are left?*

404 four hundred four   Copyright © Savvas Learning Company LLC. All Rights Reserved.   **Topic 7** | Lesson 7

Name _____

Another Look!

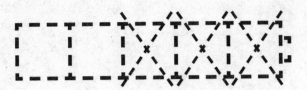

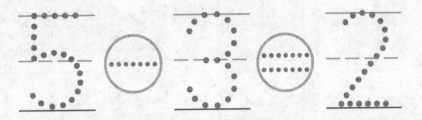

HOME ACTIVITY Give your child 7 small objects and ask him or her to give you 3 of the objects. Ask your child to tell you how many objects are left, and ask how he or she knows. Then ask your child to write an equation ($7 - 3 = 4$).

Directions Say: *There are 5 counters. 3 are taken away. How many counters are left? You can draw counters and mark Xs to show what is happening. Write an equation.* Have students listen to each story, draw pictures to show what is happening, and then write an equation. ★ *There are 6 chipmunks. 4 run under a bush. How many chipmunks are left?* ❷ *There are 5 raccoons. 2 climb up a tree. How many raccoons are left?*

❸

_____ ◯ _ _ _ ◯ _ _ _
_____   _____

♥ 4

_ _ _ ◯ _ _ _ ◯ _ _ _
        _____

✋ 5

$$6 - 5 = 1$$

☕ 6

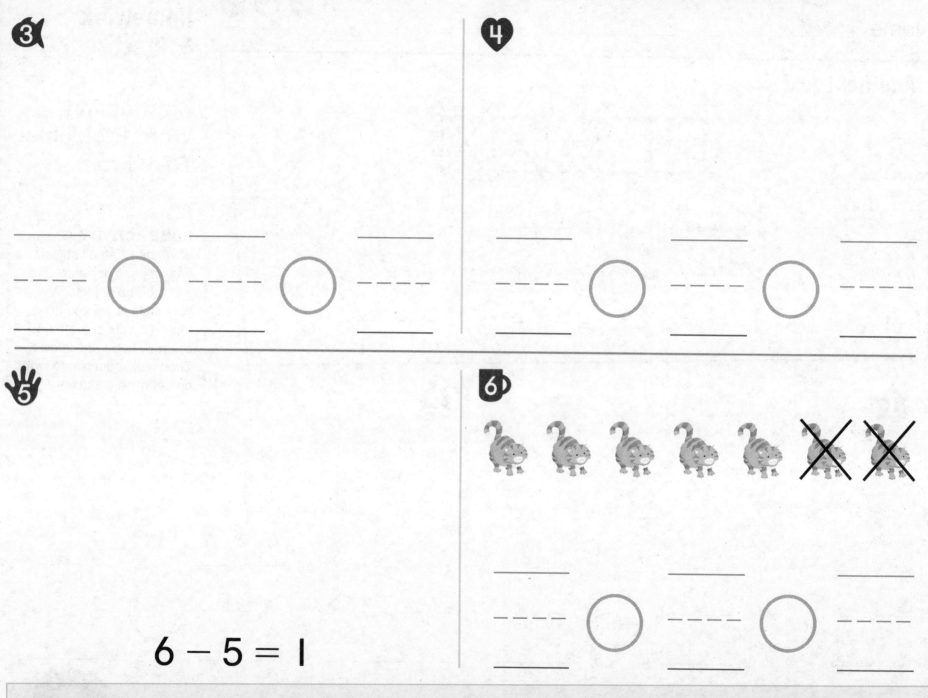

_____   _____
_ _ _ ◯ _ _ _ ◯ _ _ _

406 four hundred six

Name _____

 Solve

| 0 | 1 | 2 | 3 |

$5 - \underline{\quad} = 2$

$5 - \underline{\quad} = 3$

$5 - \underline{\quad} = \underline{\quad}$

$5 - \underline{\quad} = \underline{\quad}$

Directions Say: *Look at the first equation. Write the number from the number card that completes the equation on the orange space. Repeat for the next equation. Finish the pattern by placing the other number cards on the orange spaces, and then write the numbers to complete the equations. What patterns do you see?*

I can ... find patterns in subtraction equations.

I can also look for patterns.

$$5 - 0 = 5$$
$$5 - 1 = 4$$

$$5 - 2 = 3$$
$$5 - 3 = 2$$
$$5 - 4 = 1$$
$$5 - 5 = 0$$

$$5 - 0 = 5 \qquad 5 - 1 = 4$$
$$5 - 5 = 0 \qquad 5 - 4 = 1$$

$$5 - 2 = 3$$
$$5 - 3 = 2$$

Patterns

☆ Guided Practice

1

$$4 - 0 = \underline{\hspace{2cm}}$$

$$4 - 2 = \underline{\hspace{2cm}}$$

$$4 - 1 = \underline{\hspace{2cm}}$$

$$4 - 3 = \underline{\hspace{2cm}}$$

Directions ☆ Have students complete each equation to find the pattern, and then explain the pattern they see.

Name _____

2

3
3
3

___ − ___ = ___

___ − ___ = ___

___ − ___ = ___

3

|
|
|

___ − ___ = ___

___ − ___ = ___

___ − ___ = ___

Directions **2** and **3** Have students look for a pattern, explain the pattern they see, and then write equations for each row of insects.

Topic 7 | Lesson 8

four hundred nine **409**

Independent Practice

4

2 ___ - ___ = ___

2 ___ - ___ = ___

2 ___ - ___ = ___

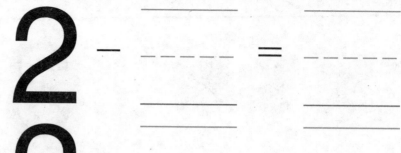

5 $10 - 6 = 4$

$10 - 4 = $ ___

6 $5 - 1 = 4$

$5 - $ ___ $ = 1$

Directions **4 Algebra** Have students mark Xs to complete the pattern, explain the pattern they see, and then write an equation for each row of flowers. **5 Higher Order Thinking** Have students find the pattern, and then complete the equation. **6 Higher Order Thinking** Have students find the pattern, and then write the missing number in the equation.

Topic 7 | Lesson 8

Help   Tools   Games

Another Look!

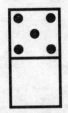 $5 - 0 = 5$

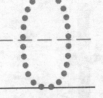

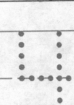 $5 - 1 = 4$

HOME ACTIVITY On a piece of paper, write: $3 - 3 = ?$; $3 - 2 = ?$; $3 - 1 = ?$; $3 - 0 = ?$. Have your child draw pictures for each problem, complete each equation, and then explain the pattern. (0, 1, 2, 3)

 $5 - \_\_\_ = \_\_\_$

 $5 - \_\_\_ = \_\_\_$

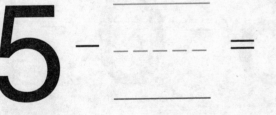

 $5 - \_\_\_ = \_\_\_$

 $5 - \_\_\_ = \_\_\_$

Directions Say: *Emily plays with dot tiles. She subtracts the side with fewer dots from the side with more dots. Write the numbers to tell how many dots are on each side, and then write how many are left after she subtracts.* ⭐ Have students use the dot tiles to complete the equations to find the pattern, and then explain the pattern they see.

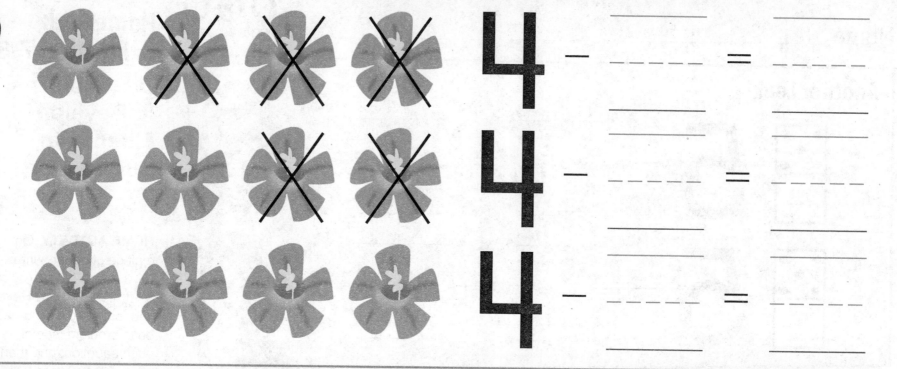

②

4 − _____ = _____

4 − _____ = _____

4 − _____ = _____

③

$$10 - 3 = 7$$

$$10 - 7 = \text{_____}$$

④

$$5 - 0 = 5$$

$$5 - \text{_____} = 0$$

Directions ② Have students mark Xs to complete the pattern, and then write an equation for each row of flowers. ③ **Higher Order Thinking** Have students find the pattern, and then complete the equation. ④ **Higher Order Thinking** Have students find the pattern, and then write the missing number in the equation.

Topic 7 | Lesson 8

Name _____

Think.

_____ _____   _____

- - - - -   ◯   - - - -   =   - - - -

_____   _____

Directions Say: *Alex has a food bar with 8 pieces of food for the flamingos at the lake. He takes apart 2 pieces of the bar to feed the flamingos. How many pieces does he have left on his bar? Use one of the tools you have to help solve the problem. Draw a picture of what you did, and then write the equation.*

I can ... use tools to subtract numbers.

I can also subtract with numbers to 9.

5 ⬤⬤⬤⬤⬤ ? — 5 ⬤⬤✖✖✖ 5 ⊙ 3 = 2 + or – ?

☆ Guided Practice

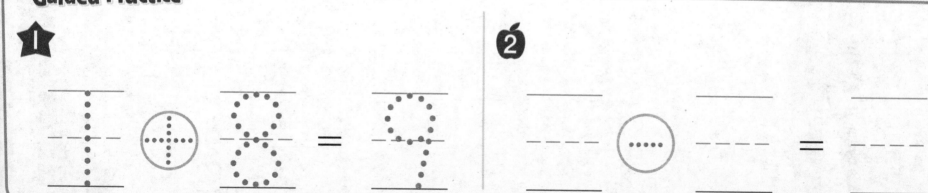

1 ⭐   I ⊕ 8 = 9

2 🍎   ___ ⊙ ___ = ___

Directions Have students listen to each story, use a tool to help them solve the problem, and then write the equation. Then have them explain whether or not the tool they chose helped to solve the problem. ⭐ *There is 1 flamingo standing in the water. 8 more fly over to join it. How many flamingos are there in all?* 🍎 *Marta sees 7 seagulls. 4 fly away. How many seagulls are left?*

Topic 7 | Lesson 9

Independent Practice

3

_ _ _ _ _ ◯ _ _ _ _ = _ _ _ _

4

_ _ _ _ _ ◯ _ _ _ _ = _ _ _ _

5

_ _ _ _ _ ◯ _ _ _ _ = _ _ _ _

6

_ _ _ _ _ ◯ _ _ _ _ = _ _ _ _

Directions Have students listen to each story, use a tool to help them solve the problem, and then write the equation. Then have them tell which tool they chose and whether or not it helped to solve the problem. **3** *There are 3 raccoons in a tree. 3 more climb the tree to join them. How many raccoons are there in all?* **4** *Marta sees 9 turtles swimming in a pond. 5 dive under the water. How many turtles are left?* **5** *There are 7 beavers in the water. 4 swim away. How many beavers are left?* **6** *Marta see 6 ducks in the lake. 2 more join them. How many ducks are there in all?*

Problem Solving

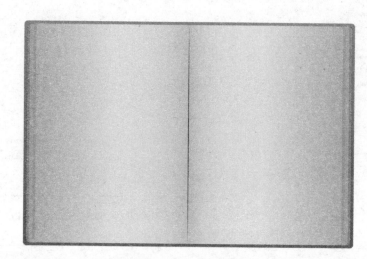

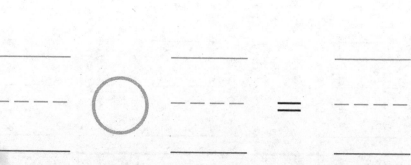

_ _ _ _ _   _ _ _ _   _ _ _ _ _

_ _ _ _   ◯   _ _ _ _   =   _ _ _ _

Directions Read the problem aloud. Then have students use multiple problem-solving methods to solve the problem. Say: *Carlos collects stamps. He has 9 stamps in all. He puts 1 stamp on the cover. He puts the rest inside the book. How many stamps does Carlos put inside his stamp book?* ♣ **Make Sense** *What are you trying to find out? Will you use addition or subtraction to solve the problem?* ⬛ **Use Tools** *What tool can you use to help solve the problem? Tell a partner and explain why.* ♦ **Be Precise** *Did you write the equation correctly? Explain what the numbers and the symbols mean in the equation.*

Name _____

Help   Tools   Games

Homework & Practice 7-9

Use Appropriate Tools

Another Look!

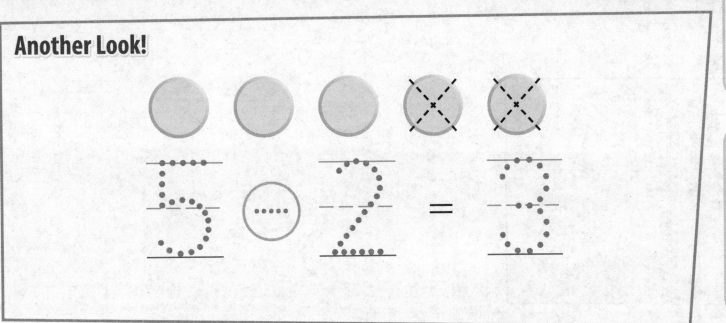

HOME ACTIVITY Give your child 5 spoons and then 2 more spoons. Ask how many there are in all. Have him or her explain whether he or she added or subtracted. Then have your child use the spoons to model the equation.

Directions Say: *You can use counters to help you decide whether a story is an addition or subtraction problem. Listen to this story:* Emily built 5 sandcastles. Waves knocked down 2 of them. How many sandcastles are left? *Model this story with counters. Did you add or subtract? Mark Xs on the counters to show subtraction, and then write the equation.* Have students listen to each story, use counters or other objects to help them solve the problem, mark Xs on the counters to show subtraction or draw counters to show addition, and then write the equation. ⭐ *Emily sees 2 balls at the beach. Later that day, she sees 3 more. How many balls does Emily see in all?* 🍎 *Emily has 6 sand shovels. Her brothers lose 3 of them. How many sand shovels are left?*

Topic 7 | Lesson 9   Digital Resources at SavvasRealize.com   four hundred seventeen   **417**

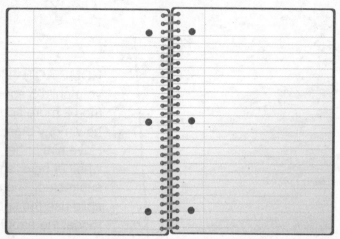

Directions Read the problem aloud. Then have students use multiple problem-solving methods to solve the problem. Say: *Emily has 7 stickers. She gives 2 to her brother. Then she sticks some stickers in her notebook. Emily has 3 stickers left. How many stickers did Emily put in her notebook?* ❸ **Make Sense** *What are you trying to find out? Will you use addition or subtraction to solve the problem?* ❹ **Use Tools** *What tool can you use to help solve the problem? Tell a partner and explain why.* ✋ **Be Precise** *Did you write the equation correctly? Explain what the numbers and the symbols mean in the equation.*

Name _____

 1

$$7 \bigcirc 5$$

 2

$$9 - 6 = 3$$

 3

_____ _____

‑ ‑ ‑ ‑ ‑   ‑ ‑ ‑ ‑ ‑

8 take away _____ is _____.

 4

_____

‑ ‑ ‑ ‑ ‑

_____

‑ ‑ ‑ ‑ ‑

Directions **Understand Vocabulary** Have students: 1 write the **minus sign** to show subtraction; 2 draw a circle around the number that tells how many are **left**; 3 complete the **subtraction sentence**; 4 **separate** the tower into 2 parts, draw each part, and then write the numbers to tell the parts.

$$8 - 3 = 5$$

Name _____

Set A

★ 1

2 are left.

_____

_ _ _ _ _ _

_____ are left.

Set B

Take apart 7.

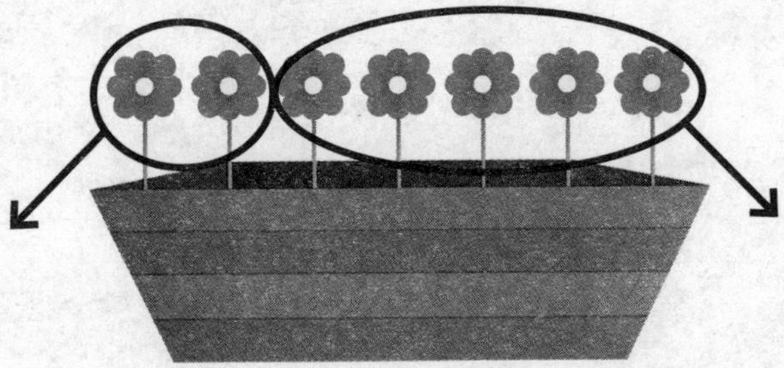

2   and   5

🍎 2

Take apart 7.

_____   _____

_ _ _ _ _   _ _ _ _ _

_____ and _____

Directions Have students: ★ count the bees, tell how many are NOT on the flower, and then write the number to tell how many are left on the flower; 🍎 take apart the group of apples. Have them draw a circle around the parts they made, and then write the numbers to tell the parts.

Topic 7 | Reteaching

four hundred twenty-one   421

Set C

8 take away 4 is 4.

③

_____   _____

_____ take away _____ is _____.

Set D

6 take away 2 is 4.

$$6 - 2 = 4$$

♥ 4

4 take away 1 is 3.

_____ ◯ _____ ◯ _____

Directions Have students: ③ listen to the story, and then complete the sentence to tell how many are left. *Javi sees 9 dragonflies. 4 fly away. How many dragonflies are left?* ④ use counters to model the problem, mark Xs to subtract, and then write an equation to find the difference.

Topic 7 | Reteaching

Name _____

$$7 - 5 = 2$$

⬤ 5

_____   ⭕   _____   ⭕   _____

_____

$$4 - 1 = 3$$

🖐 6

_____   ⭕   _____   ⭕   _____

_____

Directions Have students: 🖐 use counters to model the problem, and then write an equation to tell how many are left; 6 listen to the story, draw a picture to show what is happening, and then write an equation to match the story. *Lidia has 5 balloons. 2 balloons pop. How many balloons does she have left?*

$4 - 3 = 1$

$4 - 2 = 2$

$4 - 1 = 3$

🌲 **7**

$5 -$ _____ $=$ _____

$5 -$ _____ $=$ _____

$5 -$ _____ $=$ _____

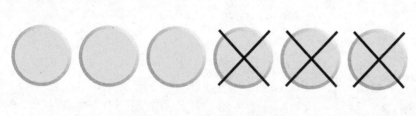

$6 - 3 = 3$

8

_____ ◯ _____ ◯ _____

_____

Directions Have students: 🌲 complete each equation to find the pattern; **8** listen to the story, use counters to help solve the problem, and then write the equation. *Darla sees 3 frogs on the pond. 7 more join them. How many frogs are there in all?*

Name _____

 1

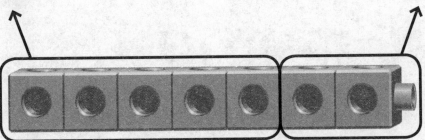

Ⓐ 6 and 2   Ⓒ 5 and 2

Ⓑ 4 and 2   Ⓓ 5 and 3

 2

Ⓐ 3   Ⓒ 5

Ⓑ 4   Ⓓ 6

3

Ⓐ 4 take away 2 is 2.   Ⓒ 3 take away 1 is 2.
   8 − 2 = 6   3 − 1 = 2

Ⓑ 4 take away 3 is 1.   Ⓓ 5 take away 3 is 2.
   4 − 3 = 1   5 − 3 = 2

 4

Ⓐ 5 − 3 = 2   Ⓒ 7 − 3 = 4

Ⓑ 5 − 2 = 3   Ⓓ 7 − 2 = 5

Directions Have students mark the best answer. 1 Which numbers tell the parts? 2 Which number tells how many are left? 3 Which sentence matches the picture? 4 Which equation matches the picture?

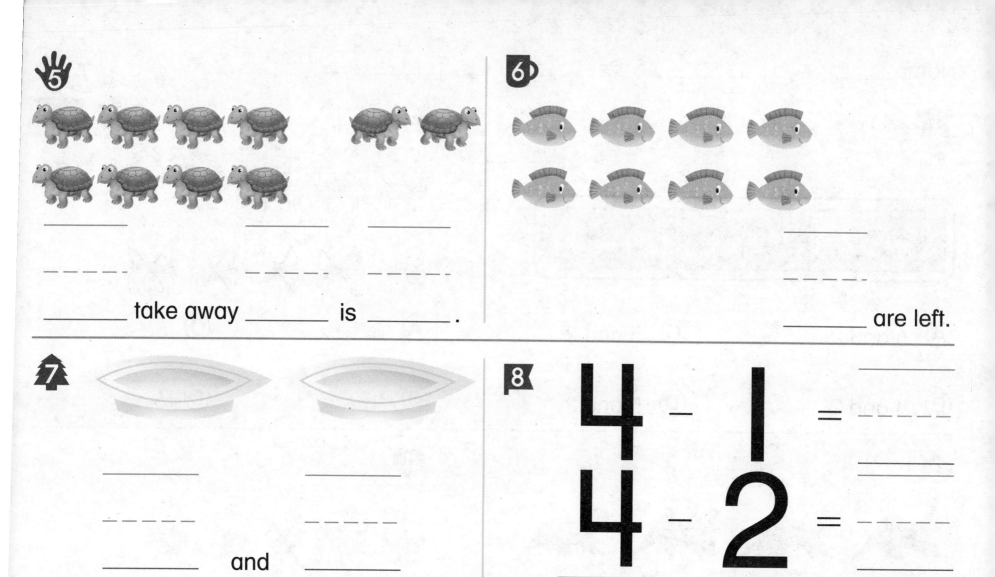

5

_____ _____ _____

- - - - - - - - - - - - - -

_____ take away _____ is _____ .

6

_____

_____ are left.

7

_____

- - - - - -

and

_____

8

4 - 1 = _____

_____

4 - 2 = - - - - -

- - - - - - - = - - - - -

_____

Topic 7 | Assessment

Name _____

9

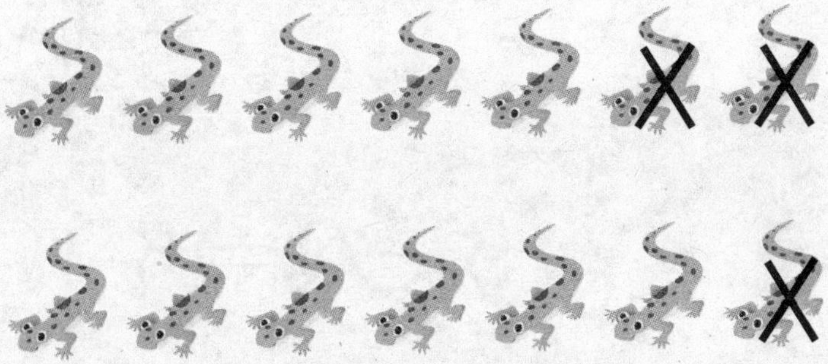

_____ ◯ - - - - ◯ - - - -
- - - - ◯ - - - - ◯ _____
_____   _____

10

Take apart 6.

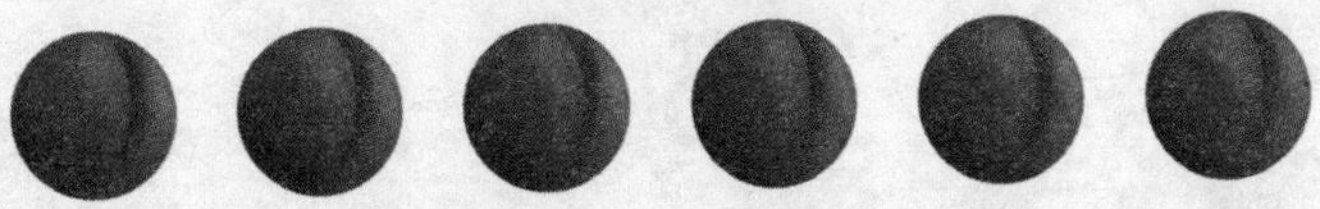

_____   _____

- - - -   - - - -

_____ and _____

❂

_____ ◯ - - - - ◯ - - - -
- - - - ◯ - - - - ◯ _____
_____   _____

$$5 - 1 = 4$$

$$5 - 0 = 5$$

$$5 - 3 = 2$$

$$5 - 4 = 1$$

$$5 - 2 = 3$$

Directions ⑫ Have students match each equation with a row of flowers to find the pattern.

Name _____

_____   _____

_ _ _ _   _ _ _ _

_____ take away _____ is _____.

$5 -\ \_\_\_\_\ =\ \_\_\_\_$

_____ _____

$5 -\ \_\_\_\_\ =\ \_\_\_\_$

_____ _____

_ _ _ _ **—** _ _ _ _ **=** _ _ _ _

_____ _____

Directions **Puppet Show** Say: *Paco's class uses many puppets for their puppet show.* ⭐ Have students listen to the story, and then write a subtraction sentence to tell how many duck puppets are left. *Paco has 8 duck puppets at school. He takes 3 home. How many duck puppets are left at school?* ❷ Write an equation to tell how many duck puppets Paco has left at school. ❸ Say: *The picture shows that Paco put 1 cat puppet in a drawer. How many cat puppets are left?* Have students write an equation for the picture, and then write another equation to complete a pattern.

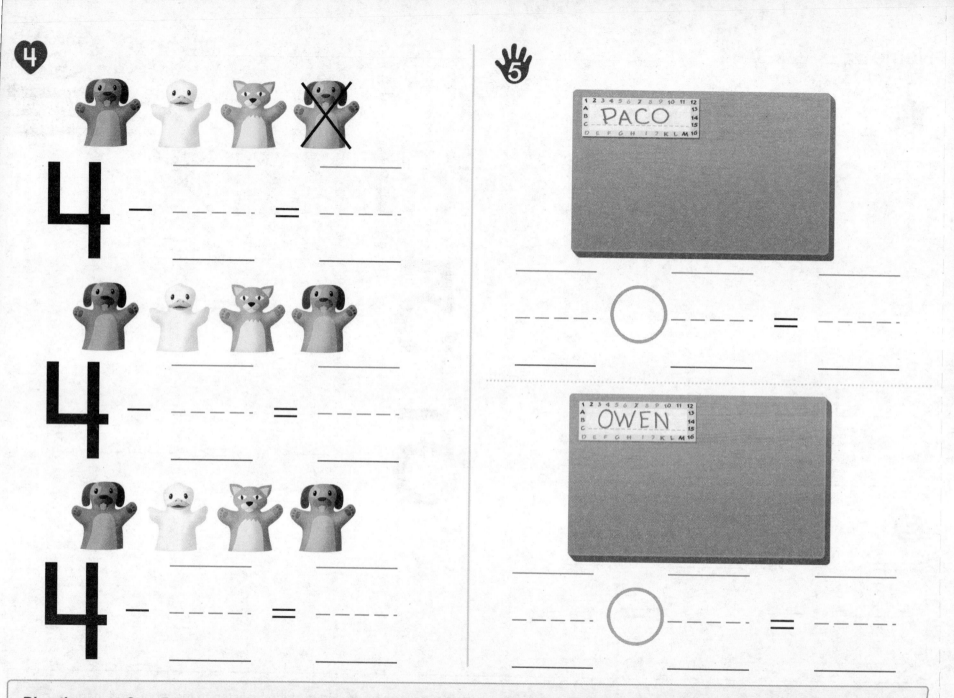

4

4 − _____ = _____

4 − _____ = _____

4 − _____ = _____

5

PACO

_____ ◯ _____ = _____

OWEN

_____ ◯ _____ = _____

Directions ♥ Say: *Paco's class puts on a play using 4 puppets. Each scene of the play has 1 more puppet leave the stage than the scene before.* Have students mark Xs to complete the pattern. Then have them write equations to show how many puppets leave each scene. ✋ Have students listen to the story, use counters to help solve each part of the problem, and then write an equation. *Paco has 4 yellow bird puppets and 3 red bird puppets on his desk. How many bird puppets does Paco have in all? Then Paco moves 2 bird puppets to his friend Owen's desk. How many bird puppets are left on Paco's desk?*

Topic 7 | Performance Assessment

More Addition and Subtraction

Essential Question: How can decomposing numbers in more than one way help you learn about addition and subtraction?

Digital Resources

Solve Learn Glossary

Tools Assessment Help Games

Look!

We can recycle.

Math and Science Project: Recycling

Directions Read the character speech bubbles to students. **Find Out!** Have students find out about the impact of littering and how recycling reduces human impact on the environment. Say: *Talk to friends and relatives about the items they recycle. Ask them how they are helping to protect the environment.* **Journal: Make a Poster** Then have students make a poster. Ask them to draw a playground littered with 4 paper, 3 plastic, and 2 metal recyclables. Have them draw a circle around the papers in green, the plastics in yellow, and the metals in orange. Finally, have students write an equation that adds the 4 paper and 3 plastic recyclables together.

Name _____

Review What You Know

 1

$$7 - 5 = 2$$

2

$$8 - 6 = 2$$

$$3 + 2 = 5$$

3

$$+ \qquad -$$

4

_____

_ _ _ _ _ _

_____

5

_____

_ _ _ _ _ _

6

_____   _____

_ _ _ _ _ _   _ _ _ _ _ _

Directions Have students: **1** draw a circle around the difference; **2** draw a circle around the subtraction equation and mark an X on the addition equation; **3** draw a circle around the minus sign; **4** and **5** count the counters, and then write the number to tell how many; **6** count the counters, and then write the numbers to tell the parts.

My Word Cards

Directions Have students cut out the vocabulary cards. Read the front of the card, and then ask them to explain what the word or phrase means.

A-Z Glossary

break apart

operation

My Word Cards

$$4 \, \textcircled{+} \, 2 = 6$$

$$4 \, \textcircled{-} \, 2 = 2$$

Point to the plus and minus signs.
Say: *The* **operation** *tells us what to do with the numbers. Addition and subtraction are types of operations.*

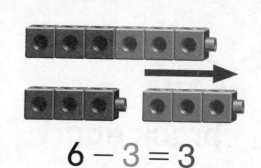

$$6 - 3 = 3$$

Point to the bottom row of blocks.
Say: *We* **break apart** *numbers to show subtraction.*

Solve & Share

Name _____

Jada's Work

My Work

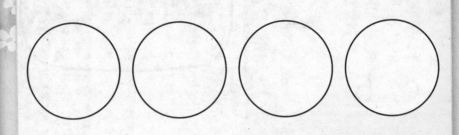

$4 = 2 + 2$

$$4 = \text{------} + \text{------}$$

Directions Say: *Jada uses yellow and red counters to show that 4 = 2 + 2. Use red and yellow counters to show a different way to take apart 4. Color to show your counters, and then write an equation to match. Tell how your work is like Jada's work and then how it is different.*

I can ...
write equations to show the parts of numbers up to 5.

I can also use math tools correctly.

Digital Resources at SavvasRealize.com

four hundred thirty-five **435**

5

2

3

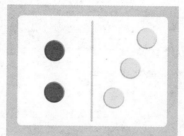

2 + 3

5 = 2 + 3

☆ Guided Practice

⭐ 1

5 = ⋮ + ⋮

Directions ⭐ Have students use yellow and red counters to show how to break apart the 5 dogs, draw a circle around each group of dogs to show a number pair for 5, and then complete the equation to show the way to break apart 5.

2 $4 = \underline{\hspace{2em}} + \underline{\hspace{2em}}$

3  $4 = \underline{\hspace{2em}} + \underline{\hspace{2em}}$

4  $4 = \underline{\hspace{2em}} + \underline{\hspace{2em}}$

Directions **2** and **3** Have students use yellow and red counters to show how to break apart the 4 cats, draw a circle around two groups of cats to show a different number pair for 4, and then complete the equation to show the way to break apart 4. **4 Math and Science** *How does pollution affect where animals live?* Have students use yellow and red counters to show how to break apart the 4 cats, draw a circle around two groups of cats to show a different number pair for 4, and then complete the equation to show the way to break apart 4.

Independent Practice

$5 = \underline{\hspace{2cm}} + \underline{\hspace{2cm}}$

$5 = \underline{\hspace{2cm}} + \underline{\hspace{2cm}}$

$5 = \underline{\hspace{2cm}} + \underline{\hspace{2cm}}$

Directions 👋 5 and 6 Have students use yellow and red counters to show how to break apart the 5 hamsters, draw a circle around two groups of hamsters to show a different number pair for 5, and then complete the equation to show the way to break apart 5. 🌲 **Higher Order Thinking** Have students draw 5 hamsters. Then have them draw a circle around two groups of hamsters to show a different number pair for 5, and then write an equation to show the way to break apart 5.

438 four hundred thirty-eight

Topic 8 | Lesson 1

Name _____

Another Look!

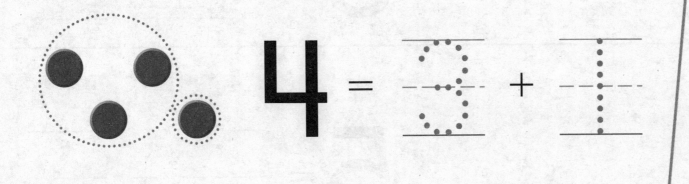

$$4 = 3 + 1$$

HOME ACTIVITY Give your child several household objects such as pennies or paper clips. Ask him or her to make a group of 4 or 5 objects. Then ask your child to break apart the objects to show pairs of 4 or 5, and then write an equation to show one way to break apart 4 or 5. Repeat this activity with a different number of objects.

$$4 = \underline{\hphantom{xxx}} + \underline{\hphantom{xxx}}$$

$$4 = \underline{\hphantom{xxx}} + \underline{\hphantom{xxx}}$$

Directions Say: *You can break apart the dots to show number pairs for 4. Draw a circle around two groups of dots. You can also write an equation to show the way to break apart 4: 4 = 3 + 1.* ⭐ and ② Have students draw a circle around two groups of dots to show a different number pair for 4, and then complete the equation to show the way to break apart 4.

3

$$5 = \underline{\hspace{2cm}} + \underline{\hspace{2cm}}$$

4

$$5 = \underline{\hspace{2cm}} + \underline{\hspace{2cm}}$$

$$\underline{\hspace{2cm}} = \underline{\hspace{2cm}} + \underline{\hspace{2cm}}$$

Directions ✦ Have students draw a circle around two groups of dots to show a different number pair for 5, and then complete the equation to show the way to break apart 5. ♥ **Higher Order Thinking** Have students draw 5 dots. Then have them draw a circle around two groups of dots to show a different number pair for 5, and then complete the equation to show the way to break apart 5. ✋ **Higher Order Thinking** Have students draw up to 5 dots. Then have them draw a circle around two groups of dots to show a different number pair for the number of dots they drew, and then write an equation to show the way to break apart the number they chose.

Name _____

Solve

$$2 + 2 = 4$$

$$4 - 2 = 2$$

Directions Say: 4 penguins play outside. 2 penguins go in the ice cave. How many penguins are left outside? Draw a circle around the equation that matches the story. Tell how you know.

I can ... solve related addition and subtraction equations.

I can also use math tools correctly.

3 + 2 = 5

Add.

5 − 2 = 3

Subtract.

☆ **Guided Practice**

Directions ⭐ Have students listen to each story and use connecting cubes to help act out each story to choose an operation. Then have students complete the equations to tell the related facts. *4 penguins are in a group. I joins them. How many penguins are there in all?* Then say: *5 penguins are in a group. I leaves. How many penguins are left?*

442 four hundred forty-two

Topic 8 | Lesson 2

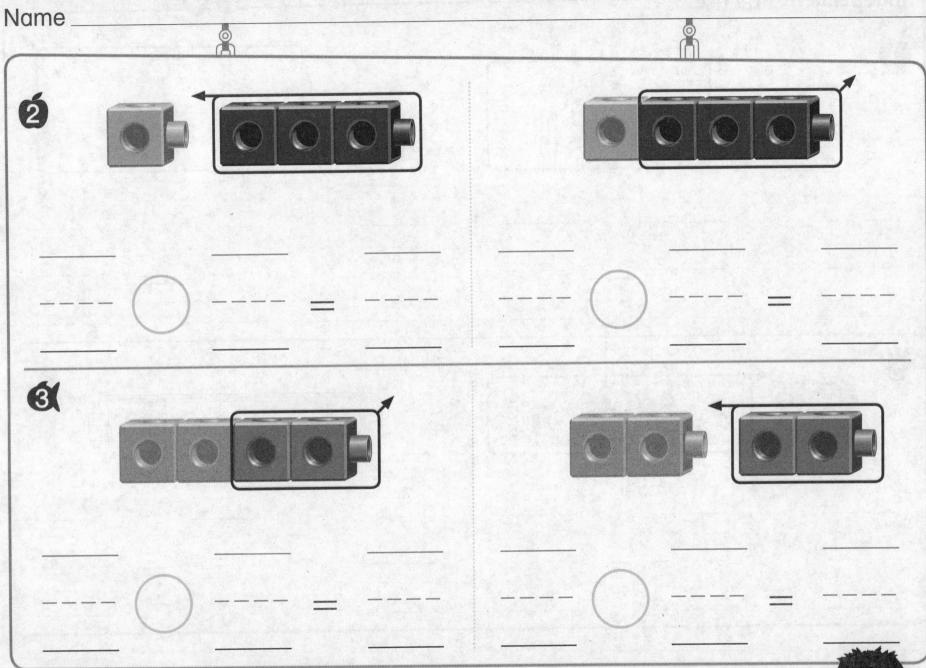

2

3

Directions ❷ and ❸ Have students use cubes for these facts with 4. Have them decide whether the cubes show addition or subtraction. Encourage students to make up their own stories to match the cubes. Then have them write equations to tell the related facts.

Independent Practice

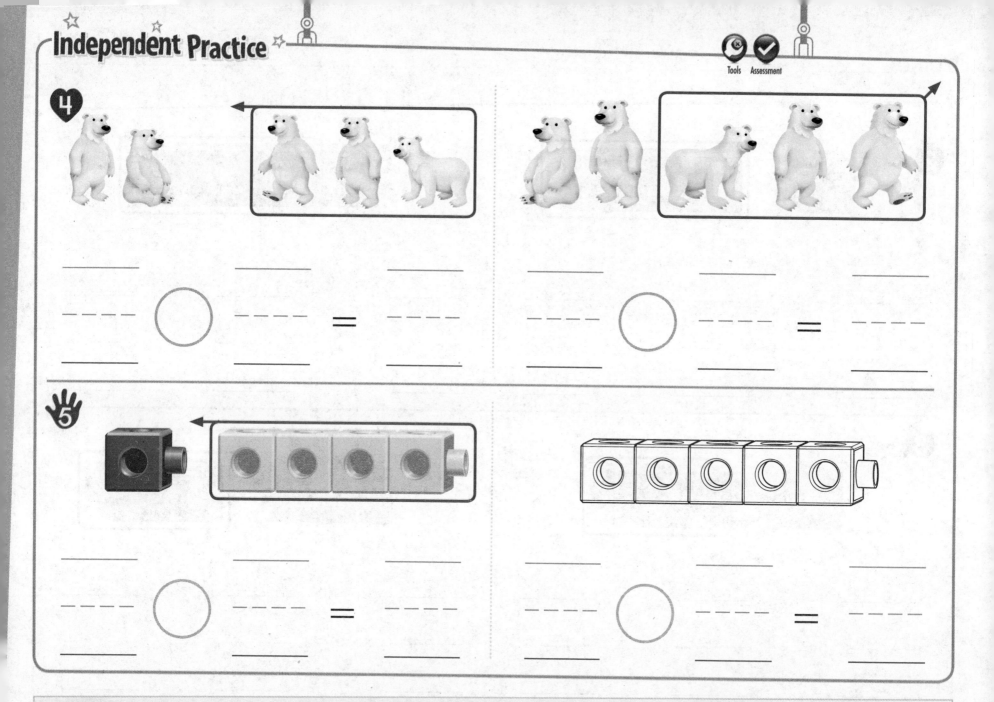

4

⬡ _____ = _____

⬡ _____ = _____

5

⬡ _____ = _____

⬡ _____ = _____

Directions ❤ Have students listen to each story, use cubes to help act out each story to choose an operation, and then write the equations to tell the related facts. *2 bears are in a group. 3 join them. How many bears are there in all?* Then say: *5 bears are in a group. 3 leave. How many bears are there now?* ✋ **Higher Order Thinking** Have students decide whether they want the cubes to show addition or subtraction, and then write an equation to match. Then have them color the cubes using the same numbers as the equation they just wrote, draw an arrow to tell the related fact, and then write the equation to match.

Name _____

Another Look!

5 ⊙ 2 = 3   3 ⊕ 2 = 5

HOME ACTIVITY Using household objects such as pennies or paper clips, ask your child to make a group of 4 or 5 objects. Then ask your child to break that group into two smaller groups and write an equation about the groups. Then have him or her write an equation to match it, using a different operation.

_ _ _ _ ◯ _ _ _ _ = _ _ _ _   _ _ _ _ ◯ _ _ _ _ = _ _ _ _

Directions Say: *Listen to each story and use counters or other objects to help act out each story to choose an operation. Then complete the equations to tell the related facts.* 5 seals are playing. 2 leave. How many seals are left? There are 3 seals playing and 2 join them. How many seals are there in all? ⭐ Have students listen to each story, use counters or other objects to help act out the story to choose an operation, and then write the equations to tell the related facts. *4 seals are in a group. 1 walks away. How many seals are left?* Then say: *3 seals are in a group. 1 joins them. How many seals are there in all?*

2

_____ _____   _____ _____

- - - ( ) - - - = - - - -   - - - ( ) - - - = - - - -

_____ _____   _____ _____

---

 3 | **4**

$4 + 1 = 5$ | $5 - 1 = 4$

Topic 8 | Lesson 2

Solve & Share

Name _____

Solve

$$4 - 2 = 2$$

Think.

Directions Say: *Jada and Carlos are at the zoo. Each of them tells a story about an animal in a habitat. How could you tell a story to match the equation shown? Tell your story to a partner.*

I can ... reason about numbers and operations.

I can also add and subtract within 5.

$$2 + 3 = ?$$

What does the + mean?

$$2 + 3 = 5$$

$$2 + 3 = 5$$

☆ Guided Practice

1

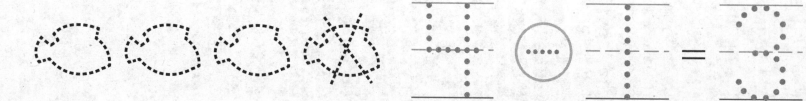

Directions ⭐ Have students tell a story for 4 − 1. Then have them draw a picture to illustrate their story and write the equation.

Tools   Assessment

Independent Practice

$$\underline{\hspace{3cm}} \quad \bigcirc \quad \underline{\hspace{2cm}} \quad = \quad \underline{\hspace{2cm}}$$

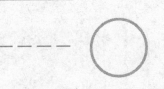

$$\underline{\hspace{3cm}} \quad \bigcirc \quad \underline{\hspace{2cm}} \quad = \quad \underline{\hspace{2cm}}$$

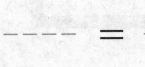 

Directions Have students tell a story for: ② 1 + 3. Then have them draw a picture to illustrate their story and write the equation; ③ 3 − 2. Then have them draw a picture to illustrate their story and write the equation.

$$4 + \underline{} = 5$$

Directions Read the problem to students. Then have them use multiple problem-solving methods to solve the problem. Say: *Carlos's teacher wrote this equation on the chalkboard:* $4 + \square = 5$. *Can you tell a story for that equation?* ✤ **Reasoning** *What story can you tell to help solve the problem and write the equation?* ✋ **Use Tools** *Does drawing a picture help to solve the problem? What does your picture show? What other tools can you use to solve the problem?* ✿ **Model** *Can a model help you solve the problem? Use the part-part model to check your answer.*

Name _____

Another Look!

HOME ACTIVITY Tell your child simple addition and subtraction stories. Have your child solve them by drawing models, such as those in the lesson, or by using his or her own representations of the problems.

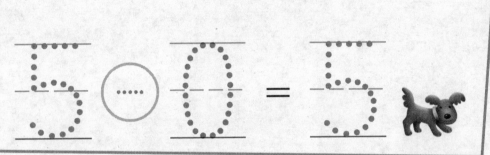

$$5 - 0 = 5$$

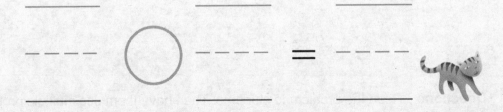

Directions Say: *You can use a picture to tell a story for 5 − 0.* Have students use the picture to tell a story, and then write the equation.
⭐ Have students tell a story for 3 − 1. Then have them draw a picture to illustrate their story and write the equation.

Topic 8 | Lesson 3   Digital Resources at SavvasRealize.com   four hundred fifty-one   **451**

② ③ ④

$$3 + 2 = \underline{}$$

Directions Read the problem to students. Then have them use multiple problem-solving methods to solve the problem. Say: *Marta's teacher challenges the class. She asks the class to tell two different stories for one equation: 3 + 2 = ☐. Can you tell two different stories for that equation?* ② **Reasoning** *What story can you tell first to help solve the problem and complete the equation?* ③ **Generalize** *What can you use from your first story to help you tell the second story? What will repeat in the second equation?* ④ **Use Tools** *Does drawing pictures help to solve the problem? What do your pictures show? What other tools can you use to solve the problem?*

Solve & Share

Name _____

Solve

___

- - - -

1 + 2 = ___

Directions Say: *Help Jada solve the equation. Solve any way you choose. Explain how you solved the problem.*

I can ... write addition and subtraction equations within 5 and remember them.

I can also be precise in my work.

Topic 8 | Lesson 4

Digital Resources at SavvasRealize.com

four hundred fifty-three **453**

$3 + 2 = ?$

$3 + 2 = 5$

$3...4, 5$

$3 - 1 = ?$

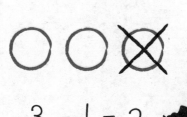

$3 - 1 = 2$

$3 - 1 = 2$

 **Guided Practice**

1

$$4 + 1 = 5$$

2

$$5 - 1 = \text{\_\_\_}$$

Directions and **2** Have students solve the equation any way they choose, and then tell how they solved the problem.

Name _____

3 2 + 1 = _____

4 3 - 1 = _____

5 2 - 2 = _____

6 1 + 4 = _____

7 4 + 0 = _____

8 4 - 2 = _____

Directions **3**–**8** Have students solve the equation any way they choose, and then tell how they solved the problem.

Topic 8 | Lesson 4　　　　　　　　　　　　　　　　four hundred fifty-five　**455**

9 $4 - 1 = \underline{\hspace{2cm}}$

10 $3 + 1 = \underline{\hspace{2cm}}$

11 $3 - 2 = \underline{\hspace{2cm}}$

12 $1 + 0 = \underline{\hspace{2cm}}$

13 $5 - 2 = \underline{\hspace{2cm}}$

14 $5 - \underline{\hspace{1.5cm}} = 5$

Directions 9–13 Have students solve the equation any way they choose, and then tell how they solved the problem. 14 **Higher Order Thinking** Have students solve for the missing number in the equation any way they choose, and then tell how they solved the problem.

Topic 8 | Lesson 4

Name _____

Another Look!

$1 + 1 = ?$

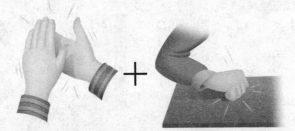

$1 + 1 =$  2

HOME ACTIVITY Show your child the equation $2 + 3 = ?$. Have him or her solve the problem any way he or she chooses. Then have your child explain how to solve the problem. Repeat for the equation $3 - 3 = ?$.

1 ⭐

$$2 + 2 = \underline{\quad}$$

2 🍎

$$2 - 1 = \underline{\quad}$$

3 🐟

$$0 + 3 = \underline{\quad}$$

4 ❤️

$$5 - 4 = \underline{\quad}$$

Directions Say: *There are many ways to solve an equation. Try clapping and knocking to solve $1 + 1$. Write the number to tell how many in all.*
⭐–❤️ *Have students solve the equation any way they choose, and then tell how they solved the problem.*

Topic 8 | **Lesson 4** Digital Resources at SavvasRealize.com four hundred fifty-seven **457**

5 $5 - 3 =$ _____

6 $1 + 3 =$ _____

7 $4 - 3 =$ _____

8 $5 + 0 =$ _____

9 $4 -$ _____ $= 2$

10 _____ $+ 4 = 4$

Directions 🖐–**8** Have students solve the equation any way they choose, and then tell how they solved the problem. **9 Higher Order Thinking** Have students solve for the missing number in the equation any way they choose, and then tell how they solved the problem. **10 Higher Order Thinking** Have students solve for the missing number in the equation any way they choose, and then tell how they solved the problem.

Name _____

Alex's Work

My Work

6 = 4 + 2

$$6 = \underline{} + \underline{}$$

Directions Say: Alex uses yellow and red counters to show that 6 = 4 + 2. Use red and yellow counters to show a different way to break apart 6. Color to show your counters, and then write an equation to match. Tell how your work is like Alex's work and then how it is different.

I can ...
write equations to show the parts of 6 and 7.

I can also use math tools correctly.

Topic 8 | Lesson 5
Digital Resources at SavvasRealize.com
four hundred fifty-nine **459**

6

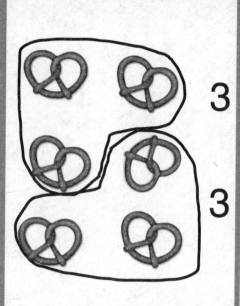

3

3

3 + 3

6 = 3 + 3

☆ Guided Practice

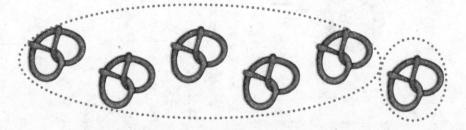

$$6 = 5 + 1$$

Directions ★ Have students use yellow and red counters to show how to break apart the 6 pretzels, draw a circle around each group of pretzels to show a number pair for 6, and then complete the equation to tell the way to break apart 6.

Topic 8 | Lesson 5

Name _____

2   **7** = _ _ _ _ _   +   _ _ _ _ _

3   **7** = _ _ _ _ _   +   _ _ _ _ _

4   **7** = _ _ _ _ _   +   _ _ _ _ _

Directions   **2–4** Have students use yellow and red counters to show how to break apart the 7 crackers, draw a circle around two groups of crackers to show a different number pair for 7, and then complete the equation to tell the way to break apart 7.

Independent Practice

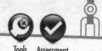

6 = _____ + _____

_____ = _____ + _____

---

6 = _____ + _____

Directions 👋 and 6️⃣ Have students use yellow and red counters to show how to break apart the 6 crackers, draw a circle around two groups of crackers to show a different number pair for 6, and then complete the equation to tell the way to break apart 6. 7️⃣ **Higher Order Thinking** Have students draw 6 crackers. Then have them draw a circle around two groups of crackers to show a different number pair for 6, and then write an equation to tell the way to break apart 6.

462 four hundred sixty-two

Topic 8 | Lesson 5

Name _____

Another Look!

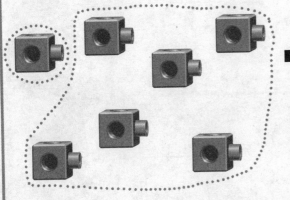

$$7 = 1 + 6$$

HOME ACTIVITY Give your child a group of objects, such as pennies, and have him or her make a group of 6 or 7. Have him or her break apart the group into two groups, and then write an equation about the objects.

 1

$$7 = \underline{\quad} + \underline{\quad}$$

2

$$7 = \underline{\quad} + \underline{\quad}$$

Directions Say: *You can break apart the cubes to show number pairs for 7. Draw a circle around two groups of cubes. You can also write an equation to tell one way to break apart 7: 7 = 1 + 6.* **1** and **2** Have students draw a circle around two groups of cubes to show a different number pair for 7, and then complete the equation to tell the way to break apart 7.

3

$6 =$ _____ $+$ _____

4

$6 =$ _____ $+$ _____

5

_____ $=$ _____ $+$ _____

Directions **3** Have students draw a circle around two groups of cubes to show a different number pair for 6, and then complete the equation to tell the way to break apart 6. **4** **Higher Order Thinking** Have students draw 6 cubes. Then have them draw a circle around two groups of cubes to show a different number pair for 6, and then complete the equation to tell the way to break apart 6. **5** **Higher Order Thinking** Have students draw 6 or 7 cubes. Then have them draw a circle around two groups of cubes to show a different number pair for the number of cubes they drew, and then write an equation to tell the way to break apart the number they chose.

Solve & Share

Name _____

 Solve

My Work

$$8 = \underline{\hspace{2cm}} + \underline{\hspace{2cm}}$$

Directions Say: *Toss 8 counters on the mat. Some land red-side up, and some land yellow-side up. Draw and color a picture of your counters, and then write an equation to match. Compare your work with a partner. How are your pictures and equations both alike and different?*

I can ... write equations to show the parts of 8 and 9.

I can also model with math.

9

5

4

5 + 4

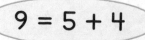

9 = 5 + 4

 9 = 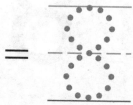 +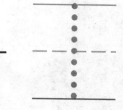

Directions ⭐ Have students use yellow and red counters to show how to break apart the 9 beets, draw a circle around two groups of beets to show a number pair for 9, and then complete the equation to tell the way to break apart 9.

466 four hundred sixty-six

Copyright © Savvas Learning Company LLC. All Rights Reserved.

Topic 8 | Lesson 6

Name _____

2

$$8 = \underline{\hspace{2cm}} + \underline{\hspace{2cm}}$$

3

$$8 = \underline{\hspace{2cm}} + \underline{\hspace{2cm}}$$

4

$$8 = \underline{\hspace{2cm}} + \underline{\hspace{2cm}}$$

Directions **2**–**4** Have students use yellow and red counters to show how to break apart the 8 peppers, draw a circle around two groups of peppers to show a different number pair for 8, and then complete the equation to tell the way to break apart 8.

Topic 8 | Lesson 6

four hundred sixty-seven **467**

Independent Practice

$$9 = \underline{\quad\quad} + \underline{\quad\quad}$$

$$9 = \underline{\quad\quad} + \underline{\quad\quad}$$

$$\underline{\quad\quad} = \underline{\quad\quad} + \underline{\quad\quad}$$

Directions and  Have students use yellow and red counters to show how to break apart the 9 pumpkins, draw a circle around two groups of pumpkins to show a different number pair for 9, and then complete the equation to tell the way to break apart 9. **Higher Order Thinking** Have students draw 9 carrots. Then have them draw a circle around two groups of carrots to show a different number pair for 9, and then complete the equation to tell the way to break apart 9.

468 four hundred sixty-eight

Topic 8 | Lesson 6

Name _____

Another Look!

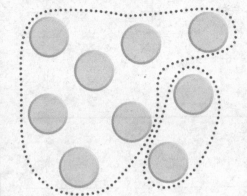

$$9 = 7 + 2$$

HOME ACTIVITY Give your child pennies, and then count 8 or 9 pennies aloud. Then have your child separate the pennies into two groups and write an equation about the pennies.

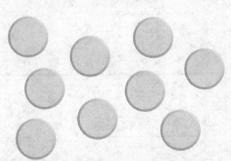

$$9 = \rule{1cm}{0.4pt} + \rule{1cm}{0.4pt}$$

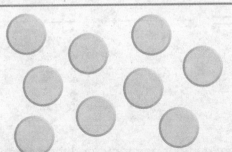

$$9 = \rule{1cm}{0.4pt} + \rule{1cm}{0.4pt}$$

Directions Say: *You can break apart the counters to show number pairs for 9. Draw a circle around two groups of counters. You can also write an equation to tell the way to break apart 9: 9 = 7 + 2.* ⭐ *and* ❷ *Have students draw a circle around two groups of counters to show a different number pair for 9, and then complete the equation to tell the way to break apart 9.*

③

$$8 = \text{\_\_\_\_} + \text{\_\_\_\_}$$

④

$$8 = \text{\_\_\_\_} + \text{\_\_\_\_}$$

$$\text{\_\_\_\_} = \text{\_\_\_\_} + \text{\_\_\_\_}$$

Solve & Share

Name _____

10 = _____ + _____   10 = _____ + _____

Directions   Say: *Jada wants to write equations to describe ways to break 10 into two parts. Draw pictures of yellow and red counters, and then write equations to tell two different ways to break apart 10.*

I can ...
write equations to show the parts of 10.

I can also model with math.

$$10 = 7 + 3$$

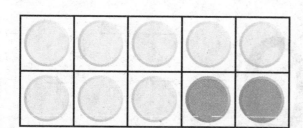

$$10 = 3 + 2$$

Directions ⭐ Have students color yellow and red counters in the ten-frame to show a number pair for 10, and then complete the equation to tell the way to break apart 10.

2

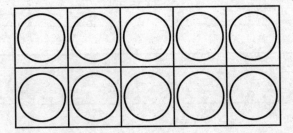

$10 = \underline{\hspace{2cm}} + \underline{\hspace{2cm}}$

3

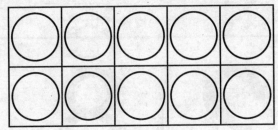

$10 = \underline{\hspace{2cm}} + \underline{\hspace{2cm}}$

4

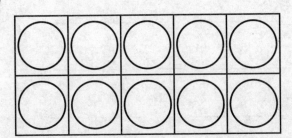

$10 = \underline{\hspace{2cm}} + \underline{\hspace{2cm}}$

Directions **2–4** Have students color yellow and red counters in the ten-frame to show a different number pair for 10, and then complete the equation to tell the way to break apart 10.

Independent Practice

 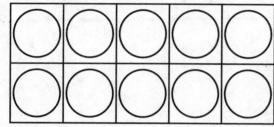

$10 = \rule{2cm}{0.4pt} + \rule{2cm}{0.4pt}$

 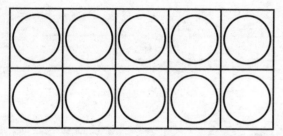

$10 = \rule{2cm}{0.4pt} + \rule{2cm}{0.4pt}$

 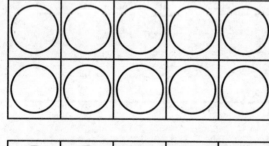

$10 = 2 + 8$

$\rule{2cm}{0.4pt} = \rule{2cm}{0.4pt} + \rule{2cm}{0.4pt}$

Directions ✋ and ☕ Have students color yellow and red counters in the ten-frame to show a different number pair for 10, and then complete the equation to tell the way to break apart 10. 🌲 **Higher Order Thinking** Have students color yellow and red counters in the top ten-frame to show the equation. Then have students write the related fact to the given equation, and then color yellow and red counters in the bottom ten-frame to match the equation they just wrote. Have students tell how the equations are both alike and different.

     Topic 8 | Lesson 7

Name _____

Another Look!

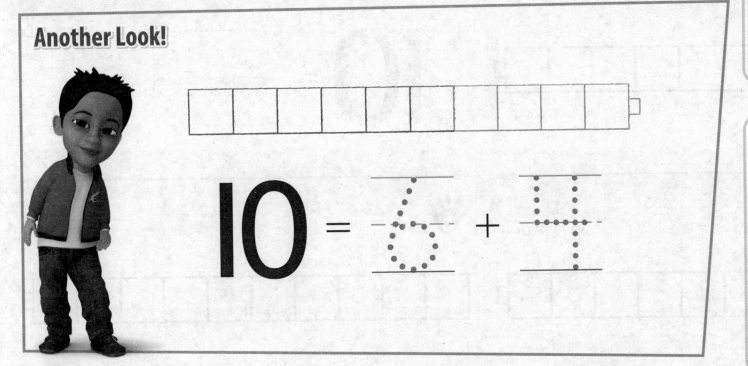

$$10 = 6 + 4$$

HOME ACTIVITY Draw 10 large circles on a piece of paper. Have your child count the number of circles. Then have him or her put household objects, such as pennies or paper clips, on some of the circles. Have your child write an equation that tells how many circles are empty and how many have objects. The equation should equal 10.

⭐ 1

$$10 = \text{\_\_\_\_} + \text{\_\_\_\_}$$

🍎 2

$$10 = \text{\_\_\_\_} + \text{\_\_\_\_}$$

Directions Say: *You can break apart the cubes to show number pairs for 10. Color the cubes to show two groups of cubes. You can also write an equation to tell the way to break apart 10: 10 = 6 + 4.* ⭐ *and* 🍎 *Have students color the cube train red and yellow to show a different number pair for 10, and then complete the equation to tell the way to break apart 10.*

③

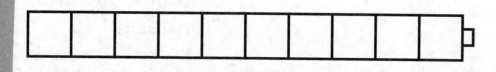

$$10 = \underline{\hspace{2cm}} + \underline{\hspace{2cm}}$$

④

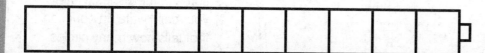

$$\underline{\hspace{2cm}} = \underline{\hspace{2cm}} + \underline{\hspace{2cm}}$$

⑤

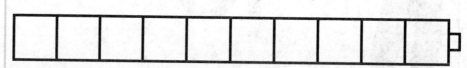

$$10 = 7 + 3$$

$$\underline{\hspace{2cm}} = \underline{\hspace{2cm}} + \underline{\hspace{2cm}}$$

Directions **③** Have students color the cube train red and yellow to show a different number pair for 10, and then complete the equation to tell the way to break apart 10. **④ Number Sense** Have students color the cube train red and yellow to show two different parts that add to 10, and then write an equation to tell the number pair. **⑤ Higher Order Thinking** Have students color the cube train red and yellow to show the equation, and then write a different equation to match the counters in the frame. Have students tell how the equations are both alike and different.

Solve & Share

Name _____

_____ + _____ = **6**

Directions Say: *Jada has 6 books she wants to place on her book shelves. Draw one way she could put her books away, and then write the number to tell how many books you drew on each shelf. Write an equation to match what you drew. Explain why your answer is correct.*

I can ... write an addition equation to solve a word problem.

I can also make sense of problems.

"7 in all"

1   6

1   6

$$7 = 1 + 6$$

☆ Guided Practice

1

$$5 = \underline{} + \underline{}$$

Directions 1 Have students listen to the story, draw circles to show breaking apart, and then complete the equation to match the story. Have them explain how they know their answers are correct. *Jorge has 5 flowers. He wants to give some of them to Shelley and some of them to Lola. How can he break apart the group of flowers?*

Name _____

2

4 = _____ + _____

3

🐚🐚🐚🐚🐚🐚🐚🐚🐚

9 = _____ + _____

4

6 = _____ + _____

Directions Have students listen to each story, draw circles to show breaking apart, and then complete the equation to match the story. Have them explain how they know their answers are correct. **2** *David has 4 marbles. He wants to give some marbles to John and some to Rob. How could he break apart the group of marbles?* **3** *Sarah has 9 seashells. She wants to give some to her brother and some to her grandfather. How can she break apart the group of shells?* **4** **Vocabulary** Say: *Nico has 6 toy owls. He wants to take some to school and leave some at home. How does he* **break apart** *the group of owls?* Complete the equation to match the story.

Independent Practice

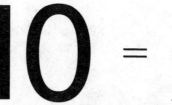

10 = _____ + _____

3 = _____ + _____

6 = _____ + _____

Directions Have students listen to each story, draw circles to show breaking apart, and then complete the equation to match the story. Then have them explain how they know their answers are correct. ✋ *Mia has 10 flowers. She wants to plant some in the garden and put some in the house. How can she take apart the group of flowers?* ☕ *Krista has 3 beach balls. She wants to give some to Allison and some to Patrick. How can she take apart the group of balls?* 🌲 **Higher Order Thinking** *Have students listen to the story, draw pictures to help solve the problem, and then complete the equation to match the story. Then have them explain how they know their answers are correct. Larry has 6 coins. He wants to give some coins to Drew and some coins to Tom. If Larry gives Drew 6 coins, how many coins does Tom get?*

 Topic 8 | Lesson 8

Name _____

Help   Tools   Games

Homework
& Practice 8-8

Solve Word
Problems:
Both Addends
Unknown

Another Look!

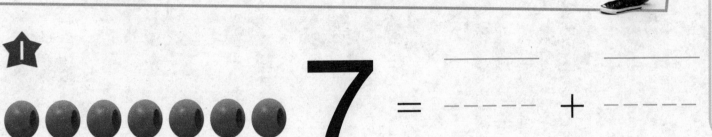

$$9 = 3 + 6$$

HOME ACTIVITY Read aloud the following problem: *A shirt has 8 buttons. The buttons are either black or white. How many buttons of each color are on the shirt?* Ask your child to draw a picture to solve the problem, and then complete the equation: ___ + ___ = 8. Repeat with different numbers of buttons.

⭐ 1

● ● ● ● ● ● ● $7 = $ ____ + ____

🍎 2

● ● ● ● ● ● ● ● $8 = $ ____ + ____

Directions   Say: *Laura has 9 beads. She uses some to make a bracelet and some to make a necklace. How can she break apart the group of beads? Complete the equation to match the story.* Then have students discuss other ways to break apart the beads. Have students listen to the story, draw circles to show breaking apart, and then complete the equation to match the story. Then have them explain how they know their answers are correct. ⭐ *Dylan has 7 beads. He wants to give some to Amy and some to Laura. How can Dylan break apart the group of beads?* 🍎 *Sharon has 8 beads. She wants to give some to Kara and some to Emma. How can Sharon break apart the group of beads?*

3

⭐ ⭐ ⭐ ⭐ $4 = \underline{\quad} + \underline{\quad}$

4

🐴 🐴 🐴 🐴 🐴 🐴 🐴 🐴 🐴

$2 + 7 = 9$ $10 = 2 + 8$ $9 = 4 + 5$ $5 + 5 = 9$

$7 + 3 = 9$ $1 + 8 = 9$ $6 + 3 = 9$ $8 = 5 + 3$

Directions ❸ Have students listen to the story, draw circles to show breaking apart, and then complete the equation to match the story. *Andrew has 4 sea stars. He gives some to Danny and some to Alisa. How can he break apart the group of sea stars?* ❹ **Higher Order Thinking** Have students listen to the story, and then mark an X on the equations that are NOT answers to the story. Ask them to explain how they know which equations are answers and which are NOT answers. *Logan has 9 sea horse stickers. He wants to put some on his folder and some on his notebook. How can he break apart the group of stickers?*

 Topic 8 | Lesson 8

Solve & Share

Name _____

Solve

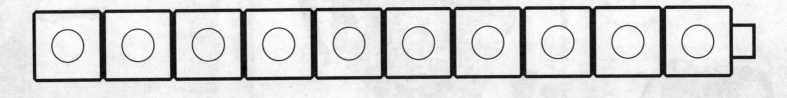

_____ + _____ = 10

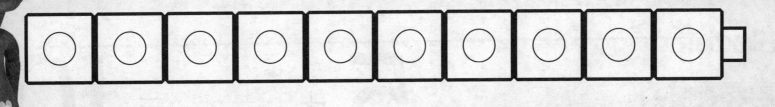

_____ + _____ = 10

Directions Say: *Use red and blue cubes to make two different trains. Each train should have 10 cubes. Use blue and red crayons to color the cube trains you made. Then write the missing numbers in the equation for each cube train.*

I can ... find number partners for 10.

I can also model with math.

☆ Guided Practice

1 $5 + 5 = 10$

2 $9 + \_\_ = 10$

Directions Have students: **1** count the red cubes to find one part of 10, use blue cubes to find the number under the cover, and then write the missing number in the equation to tell the parts of 10; **2** count the blue cubes to find one part of 10, use red cubes to find the number under the cover, and then write the missing number in the equation to tell the parts of 10.

 Topic 8 | Lesson 9

Name _____

❸ $7 + \underline{\hspace{2cm}} = 10$

❹ $2 + \underline{\hspace{2cm}} = 10$

✋5 $6 + \underline{\hspace{2cm}} = 10$

☕6 $5 + \underline{\hspace{2cm}} = 10$

Directions Have students: ❸ count the red cubes to find one part of 10, use blue cubes to find the number under the cover, and then write the missing number in the equation to tell the parts of 10; ❹ count the blue cubes to find one part of 10, use red cubes to find the number under the cover, and then write the missing number in the equation to tell the parts of 10; ✋5 and ☕6 count the straight fingers to find one part of 10, use their own fingers to find the other part, and then write the missing number in the equation to tell the parts of 10.

Independent Practice

7

$$4 + \underline{} = 10$$

8

$$8 + \underline{} = 10$$

9

$$1 + \underline{} = 10$$

10

$$\underline{} + \underline{} = 10$$

Directions 7–9 Have students draw a picture to show the parts of 10, and then write the missing number in the equation to tell the parts of 10. **10 Higher Order Thinking** Say: *A child is holding up 3 fingers to show how old she is. What part of 10 is she showing? Use that number to write the missing numbers in the equation to tell the parts of 10.*

486 four hundred eighty-six

Topic 8 | Lesson 9

Name _____

Another Look!

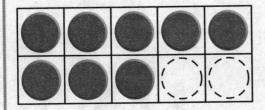

$$8 + 2 = 10$$

1

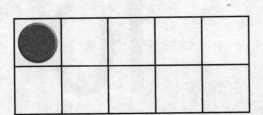

$$4 + \text{\_\_\_\_} = 10$$

2

$$1 + \text{\_\_\_\_} = 10$$

Directions Say: *You can show parts of 10 with counters and a ten-frame. Draw the missing part of 10, and then write the missing number in the equation to tell the parts of 10.* ★ *and* ❷ *Have students count the red counters to find one part of 10, draw the yellow counters to show the other part, and then write the missing number in the equation to tell the parts of 10.*

3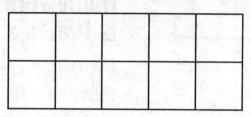

$$5 + \underline{\hspace{2cm}} = 10$$

4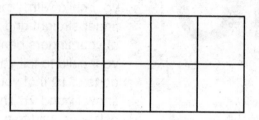

$$7 + \underline{\hspace{2cm}} = 10$$

5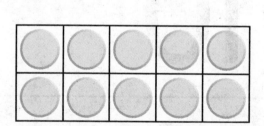

$$\underline{\hspace{1.5cm}} + \underline{\hspace{1.5cm}} = 10$$

$$\underline{\hspace{1.5cm}} + \underline{\hspace{1.5cm}} = 10$$

488 four hundred eighty-eight

Topic 8 | Lesson 9

Directions Say: *Jada visits a farm. The owner says there are 10 goats on the farm. Jada only sees 8 goats. How many are inside the barn? Draw pictures of the goats that are in the barn, and then tell how you know.*

I can ... find a missing part to make 10.

I can also model with math.

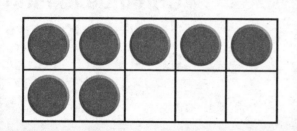

$$7 + ? = 10$$

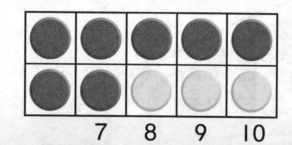

7 8 9 10

3 yellow counters

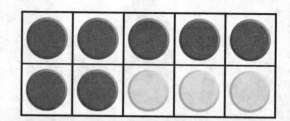

$$7 + 3 = 10$$

☆ Guided Practice

 1

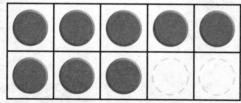

$$8 + 2 = 10$$

2

$$5 + \underline{} = 10$$

Directions **1**–**2** Have students draw yellow counters in the ten-frame to find the missing part of 10, and then write the missing number in the equation.

490 four hundred ninety

Name _____

$9 + \underline{} = 10$

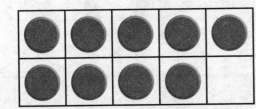

$4 + \underline{} = 10$

$2 + \underline{} = 10$

$1 + \underline{} = 10$

Directions ❸–❻ **Algebra** Have students draw yellow counters in the ten-frame to find the missing part of 10, and then write the missing number in the equation.

Independent Practice

 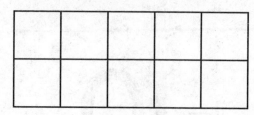 $3 + \underline{} = 10$

 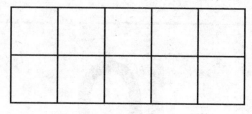 $5 + \underline{} = 10$

 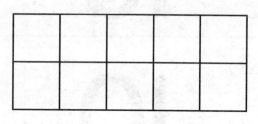 $0 + \underline{} = 10$

$$5 + 5 = 10 \qquad 5 + 6 = 10 \qquad 9 + 2 = 10 \qquad 9 + 1 = 10$$

Directions ⭐–◆ Have students draw counters in the ten-frame to show the part that they know, and then draw yellow counters in the empty spaces in the ten-frame and count to find the missing part of 10. Then have students write the missing number in the equation.
⌂ **Higher Order Thinking** Have students mark an X on the two equations that are NOT true. Then have them explain how they know which equations are true and which are NOT true.

Name _____

Help Tools Games

Homework & Practice 8-10

Continue to Find the Missing Part of 10

Another Look! 6 + ? = 10

6, ____, ____, ____, 10

6 + ☐ = 10

4 numbers

HOME ACTIVITY Give your child 7 small objects such as coins or beans. Ask your child to add objects until he or she has 10 objects. Then have your child fill in the missing number in this equation: 7 + ? = 10 (3). Repeat the activity by starting with groups of 5, 8, and 9 objects.

⭐ 1

🍎 2

9 + ____ = 10   2 + ____ = 10

Directions Say: *You can count on to find the missing part of 10. Count on from 6 until you reach 10. How many numbers did you count? Write the missing number in the equation.* ⭐–🍎 Have students show how to count on to find the missing part of 10, and then write the missing number in the equation. Then have them explain how they know their answer is correct.

Topic 8 | Lesson 10

Digital Resources at SavvasRealize.com

four hundred ninety-three **493**

3 $7 + \underline{\hspace{2cm}} = 10$

4 $5 + \underline{\hspace{2cm}} = 10$

5 $1 + \underline{\hspace{2cm}} = 10$

6 $10 + \underline{\hspace{2cm}} = 10$

7 $\underline{\hspace{2cm}} + \underline{\hspace{2cm}} = 10$

8 $\underline{\hspace{2cm}} + \underline{\hspace{2cm}} = \underline{\hspace{2cm}}$

494 four hundred ninety-four

⭐ 1

1 + 2	5 − 2	4 − 1	3 + 0	3 − 0
5 − 3	4 + 1	0 + 3	2 + 2	1 + 0
2 − 1	5 − 4	5 − 2	0 + 0	1 + 4
3 + 2	3 − 1	4 − 1	5 − 1	4 − 0
3 − 3	2 + 0	2 + 1	2 + 3	1 + 1

🍎 2

_____

_ _ _ _ _ _ _

_____

Directions Have students: ⭐ color each box that has a sum or difference that is equal to 3; 🍎 write the letter that they see.

I can ...
add and subtract fluently to 5.

⭐

$$10 - 5 = 5$$

 ②

$$6 + 3 = 9$$

 ③

$$8 \bigcirc 7 = \underline{}$$

 ④

 $9 = \underline{} \bigcirc \underline{}$

Directions **Understand Vocabulary** Have students: ⭐ draw a circle around the **minus sign**; ② draw a circle around the **sum**; ③ complete the number sentence and find the **difference**; ④ show a way to **break apart** the number by drawing one part in the box and one part outside the box. Then have them write an equation to tell how the whole was broken into two parts.

Name _____

Set A

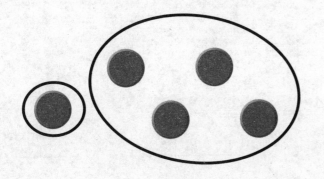

$$5 = 1 + 4$$

⭐ 1

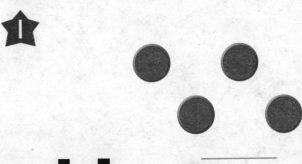

$$4 = \underline{\quad} + \underline{\quad}$$

Set B

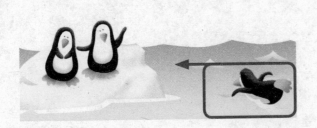

$$2 + 1 = 3$$

🍎 2

$$\underline{\quad} \bigcirc \underline{\quad} = \underline{\quad}$$

Directions Have students: ⭐ use yellow and red counters to show how to break apart the 4 counters, draw a circle around two groups of counters to show a number pair for 4, and then complete the equation to show the way to break apart 4; 🍎 listen to the story, and then use connecting cubes to help act out the story to choose an operation. Then have students complete the equation to show the related fact for $2 + 1 = 3$. *3 penguins are in a group. 1 leaves. How many penguins are left?*

$$4 + 1 = 5$$

$$5 - 3 = 2$$

$$3 + 1 = \underline{\hspace{1cm}}$$

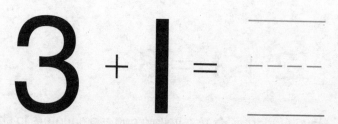

Directions Have students: ❸ tell a story for 4 – 3. Then have them draw a picture to illustrate their story and write the equation. ❹ solve the equation in any way they choose, and then tell how they solved the problem.

Name _____

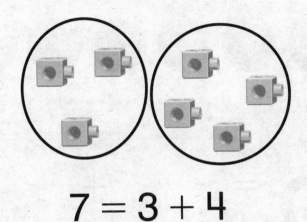

$7 = 3 + 4$

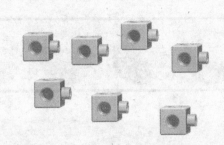

$7 = $ _ _ _ _ + _ _ _ _

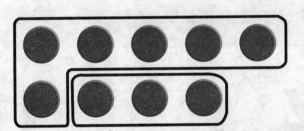

$9 = 6 + 3$

$9 = $ _ _ _ _ + _ _ _ _

Directions Have students: ✋ use yellow and red counters to show how to break apart the 7 cubes, draw a circle around two groups of cubes to show a number pair for 7, and then complete the equation to show the number pair; ☕ use yellow and red counters to show how to break apart the 9 counters, draw a circle around two groups of counters to a show number pair for 9, and then complete the equation to show the number pair.

$$5 = 1 + 4$$

$$6 = \underline{\hspace{2em}} + \underline{\hspace{2em}}$$

$$1 + 9 = 10$$

8

$$6 + \underline{\hspace{2em}} = 10$$

Directions Have students: 🎄 listen to the story, draw circles around each group to show breaking apart, and then complete the equation to match the story. *Bridget has 6 marbles. She gives some to Jessica and some to Christopher. How can she break apart the group of marbles?* 🚩 count the green cubes to find one part of 10, use yellow cubes to find the number under the cover, and then complete the equation to show the parts of 10.

 Topic 8 | Reteaching

Name _____

 1

Ⓐ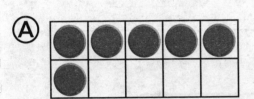

Ⓒ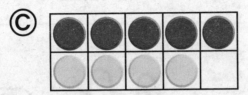

Ⓑ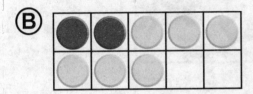

Ⓓ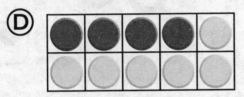

 2

Ⓐ $7 = 2 + 5$ Ⓒ $7 = 6 + 1$

Ⓑ $7 = 3 + 4$ Ⓓ $8 = 3 + 5$

 3

☐ $2 + 6 = 8$ ☐ $4 + 4 = 8$

☐ $3 + 5 = 8$ ☐ $5 + 3 = 8$

 4

☐ $2 + 6 = 8$ ☐ $2 + 7 = 9$

☐ $3 + 6 = 9$ ☐ $6 + 3 = 9$

Directions Have students mark the best answer. ★ Which shows one way to break apart 10? ② Which equation matches the picture? ③ Look at the picture. Mark all the equations that describe the picture. ④ Have students listen to the story, and then mark all the equations that show possible solutions. *Valentina buys 9 beads to make a bracelet. Some beads are blue and some are purple. How many blue beads and how many purple beads did she use so that there are exactly 9 beads in the bracelet?*

$5 =$ _____ $+$ _____

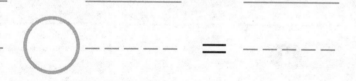

_____ $\bigcirc$ _____ $=$ _____   _____ $\bigcirc$ _____ $=$ _____

_____ $\bigcirc$ _____ $=$ _____

Directions Have students: use yellow and red counters to show how to break apart the 5 snails, draw a circle around the groups of snails to show a number pair for 5, and then complete the equation to show the way to break apart 5; listen to each story, use connecting cubes to help act out each story to choose an operation, and then write the equations to show the related facts. *2 penguins are in a group. 3 join them. How many penguins are there in all?* Then say: *5 penguins are in a group. 3 leave. How many penguins are left?* tell a story for 5 − 4. Then have them draw a picture to illustrate their story and write the equation.

Name _____

8 $6 =$ _____ $+$ _____

9 $8 =$ _____ $+$ _____

10 $5 =$ _____ $+$ _____

Directions Have students: **8** draw a circle around two groups of cars to show number pairs for 6, and then complete the equation to show the number pair; **9** draw a circle around two groups of onions to show number pairs for 8, and then complete the equation to show the number pair; **10** listen to the story, draw circles to show breaking apart, and then write the numbers in the equation to match the groups they drew circles around. *Marco has 5 flowers. He gives some to his mom and some to his grandmother. How can he break apart the group of flowers?*

_____ _____
- - - - - + - - - - - = **10**
_____ _____

---

⑫

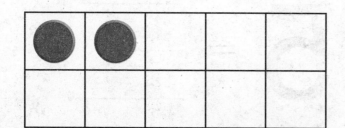

10 = _____ _____
- - - - - + - - - - -
_____ _____

---

⑬

_____
2 + - - - - - = **10**
_____

⭐ 1

$$7 = \text{-----} + \text{-----}$$

$$7 = \text{-----} + \text{-----}$$

🍎 2

$$\text{-----} = \text{-----} + \text{-----}$$

🐟 3

$$\text{-----} + \text{-----} = 5$$

$$\text{-----} + \text{-----} = 5$$

$$5 - \text{-----} = \text{-----}$$

$$5 - \text{-----} = \text{-----}$$

Directions **Fern's Farmstand** Say: *Fern sells different fruits and vegetables at her farmstand.* Have students look at the: ⭐ carrots and cucumbers Fern has at her farmstand, and then write two equations to describe them; 🍎 lettuce and radishes Fern has at her farmstand, and then write an equation to describe them; 🐟 red and green peppers that Fern is selling at her farmstand. Have students tell a story about them, and then write the missing numbers in the equation for their story. Then have students write the missing numbers in the other three equations.

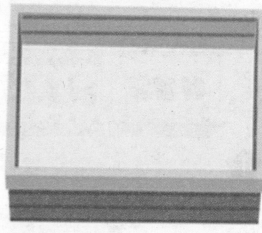

10 = _____ + _____

10 = _____ + _____

9

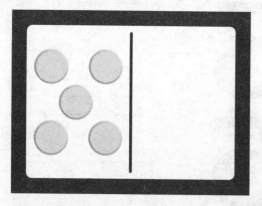

_____ ◯ _____ = _____

Topic 8 | Performance Assessment

Glossary

A

above

 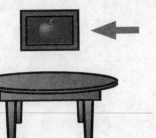

add

$$3 + 2 = 5$$

addition sentence

3 and 5 is 8.

attribute

B

balance scale

behind

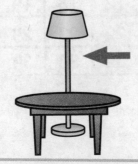

below

beside

break apart

$$6 - 3 = 3$$

capacity

category

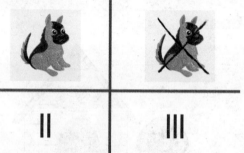

chart

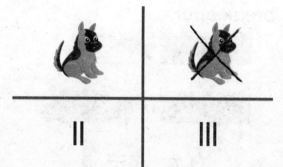

circle

classify

column

I	2	3	4	5
11	12	13	14	15
21	22	23	24	25
31	32	33	34	35

compare

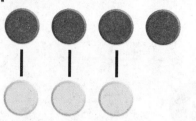

cone

count

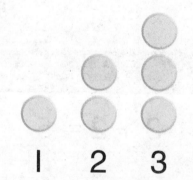

1   2   3

cube

cylinder

D

decade

1	2	3	4	5	6	7	8	9	10
11	12	13	14	15	16	17	18	19	20
21	22	23	24	25	26	27	28	29	30
31	32	33	34	35	36	37	38	39	40
41	42	43	44	45	46	47	48	49	50
51	52	53	54	55	56	57	58	59	60
61	62	63	64	65	66	67	68	69	70
71	72	73	74	75	76	77	78	79	80
81	82	83	84	85	86	87	88	89	90
91	92	93	94	95	96	97	98	99	100

difference

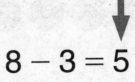

$$8 - 3 = 5$$

E

eight

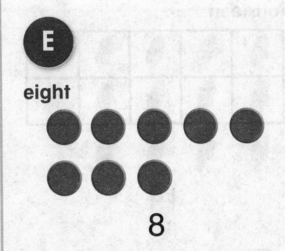

8

eighteen

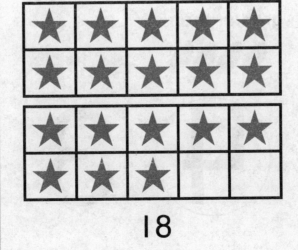

18

eleven

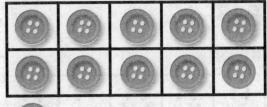

11

equal

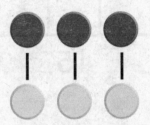

equal sign (=)

$$4 + 3 = 7$$

equation

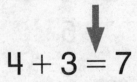

$$5 + 3 = 8$$

$$8 = 8$$

fifteen

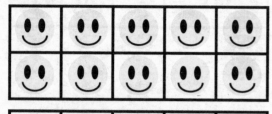

15

five

5

flat surface

four

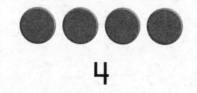

4

fourteen

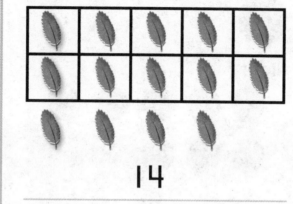

14

G

greater than

group

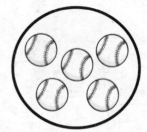

H

heavier

height

hexagon

How many more?

hundred chart

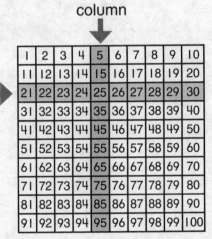

column

row →

1	2	3	4	5	6	7	8	9	10
11	12	13	14	15	16	17	18	19	20
21	22	23	24	25	26	27	28	29	30
31	32	33	34	35	36	37	38	39	40
41	42	43	44	45	46	47	48	49	50
51	52	53	54	55	56	57	58	59	60
61	62	63	64	65	66	67	68	69	70
71	72	73	74	75	76	77	78	79	80
81	82	83	84	85	86	87	88	89	90
91	92	93	94	95	96	97	98	99	100

I

in all

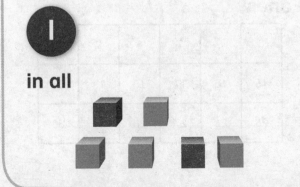

in front of

J

join

L

left

length

less than

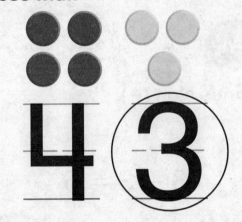

4 3

lighter

longer

M

minus sign (−)

$$8 - 3 = 5$$

model

8

N

next to

nine

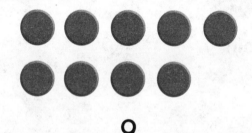

9

nineteen

19

none

0

number

0   1   2   3   4   5

O

one

1

ones

5	6	7	8	9	10
15	16	17	18	19	20
25	26	27	28	29	30

operation

$$4 \oplus 2 = 6$$
$$4 \ominus 2 = 2$$

order

$$0 \rightarrow 1 \rightarrow 2 \rightarrow 3 \rightarrow 4 \rightarrow 5$$

part

pattern

10 20 30 40 50

plus sign (+)

$$3 + 1 = 4$$

 R

rectangle

roll

row

1	2	3	4	5
11	12	13	14	15
21	22	23	24	25
31	32	33	34	35

 S

same number as

separate

seven

7

seventeen

17

shorter

side

six

6

sixteen

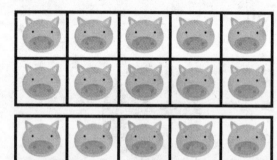

16

slide

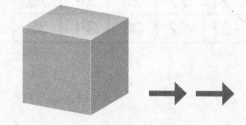

sort

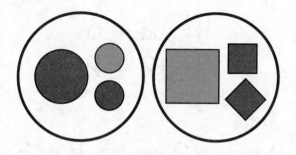

sphere

square

stack

subtract

$$3 - 1 = 2$$

subtraction sentence

4 take away 3 is 1.

sum

$$2 + 3 = 5$$

take away

taller

tally mark

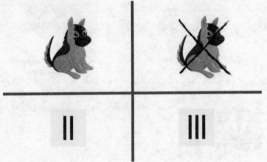

II   III

ten

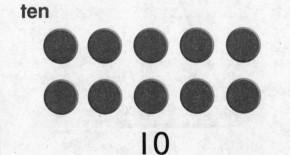

10

tens

5	6	7	8	9	10
15	16	17	18	19	20
25	26	27	28	29	30

thirteen

13

three

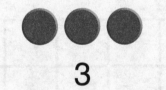

3

three-dimensional shape

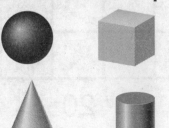

triangle

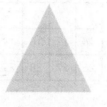

twelve

12

twenty

20

two

2

two-dimensional shape

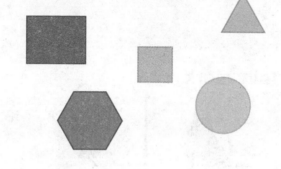

V

vertex/vertices

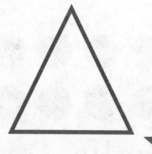

W

weighs

weight

whole

Z

zero

0

Photographs

Photo locators denoted as follows: Top (T), Center (C), Bottom (B), Left (L), Right (R), Background (Bkgd)

001 Jorge Salcedo/Shutterstock;**085L** Evgeny Murtola/Shutterstock;**085R** 2rut/Shutterstock;**135** Michal Kolodziejczyk/Fotolia;**199** James Insogna/Fotolia;**245** Christopher Elwell/Shutterstock;**281** tankist276/Shutterstock;**359** Shutterstock;**431** Winai Tepsuttinun/Shutterstock;**507** Panda3800/Shutterstock;**563** Turbojet/Shutterstock;**621** Andrey Pavlov/Shutterstock;**675** Eugene Sergeev/Shutterstock;**745** Michael Flippo/Fotolia;**799** Singkham/Shutterstock.